IMAGES
of America

CINCINNATI CEMETERIES
THE QUEEN CITY UNDERGROUND

One ghostly eye is all that remains of the face on little Carrie Hurley's statue. The marble monument in Spring Grove Cemetery shows a macabre mask eroded by urban pollution and the weather. Forever clad in her sash and dress, her tiny hand clutching a bouquet of flowers, Carrie presents a graphic spectre of the dead.

IMAGES
of America

CINCINNATI CEMETERIES
THE QUEEN CITY UNDERGROUND

Kevin Grace and Tom White

ARCADIA
PUBLISHING

Published by Arcadia Publishing
Charleston, South Carolina

Library of Congress Catalog Card Number: 2004110525

For all general information contact Arcadia Publishing at:
Telephone 843-853-2070
Fax 843-853-0044
E-mail sales@arcadiapublishing.com
For customer service and orders:
Toll-Free 1-888-313-2665

Visit us on the Internet at www.arcadiapublishing.com

(*Cover image*) Vine Street Hill Cemetery, photograph by Tom White.

CITY HOSPITAL, CINCINNATI, OHIO.

After helping gain a state charter in 1819 to open the Medical College of Ohio, founder Daniel Drake, a physician and scientist, realized that an essential part of learning medicine was first-hand experience with the sick and dying. So, he obtained another charter in 1823, this time to establish the Commercial Hospital and Lunatic Asylum. Drake was a cantankerous sort who began several medical schools only to be booted from them by a faculty that couldn't get along with him. But he was a brilliant man and knew clinical experience in a teaching hospital would benefit medical students. This early 1900s view is of the successor to his "asylum," Cincinnati's City Hospital, which later became General Hospital and is now University Hospital.

CONTENTS

Acknowledgments   6

Introduction   7

1.   Reaching the End of the Line:
         Death and Dying in Cincinnati   9

2.   Beauty and Remembrance:
         Spring Grove Cemetery   23

3.   Testaments of Time:
         Notable Cemeteries and Monuments   45

4.   Our Dearly Departed:
         Cincinnatians Worth Knowing   77

Notes for Further Reading   127

ACKNOWLEDGMENTS

Thanks for assistance and information to Kate Barone, Greg Hand, Linda Hand, Anna Heran, Steven Schwartz, Don Heinrich Tolzmann, Joe Wendt of New St. Joseph's Cemetery, the staff of the Cincinnati Historical Society with special thanks to Tina Bamert, our editor at Arcadia, Melissa Basilone, for her patience and encouragement, and all the Cincinnati cemetery employees who maintain the physical environments that offer inspiration to those who visit and comfort to those who mourn.

Thanks to my wife, Michelle, for her caring support and valuable assistance, not only during the preparation of this work but every day for the past 31 years, and to our 12-year old daughter Anna, who, after an exhaustive search for Buck Ewing's grave in Mt. Washington Cemetery, exclaimed, "I think people should be buried in alphabetical order!" I dedicate this book to the memory of my great-grandfather, Charles A. Gardner, who for many years served as sexton of Maplewood Cemetery in Ripley, Ohio.

T.W.

Thanks to my wife, Joan Fenton, who always embraces every book idea with cheer and useful advice, and my children, Courtney, Josh, and Sean, who received both history and driving lessons in Spring Grove Cemetery, and Bonnie and Lily, soon to follow their older brothers and sister in hearing their dad talk about turn signals and tombstones. And, here's to all the Graces of Emmetsburg, Iowa, who lived and died with simplicity and dignity.

K.G.

INTRODUCTION

No aspect of our culture gives rise to more tales, anecdotes, scandals, and memories than the subject of death. Eventually it is the topic we all have in common. What happens immediately before and forever after defines how we regard our history and our fellow man. And, what we end up thinking of the dead isn't always objective. The pious and overwrought epitaphs found in graveyards once moved writer Olin Miller to remark, "Reading tombstones always makes me wonder where they bury folks that ain't going to heaven."

However we view death, either our own or that of our neighbors and loved ones, is determined by every aspect of our society—faith, occupation, family, and community. These are the elements of human interaction that determine how we approach sickness and health. And if health is merely the slowest rate at which one can die, then everything will finally come to bear on those moments when we breathe our last.

The heritage of death and dying in Cincinnati has encompassed everything from the Victorian fascination with Egyptian art and sculpture to the issues of race and ethnicity requiring separate graveyards for separate groups of people. We hear stories, like the tale of a church in an old city neighborhood where the sub-basement is paved with the gravestone slabs of the abandoned cemetery on which it stands or Music Hall, standing in part on a long-gone potter's field whose ghosts rise to harass concert-goers and performers. And, this local history contains elements that reflect the growth of the city and an unusual combination of crime and education. In the 19th century, for example, Cincinnati was home to nearly a score of medical schools, most of which had some need for anatomy instruction. In a city teeming with the arrivals of immigrants and transients, a city also filled with blocks of saloons and its share of intoxicated patrons, the curious industry of body snatching took advantage of these opportunities and made Cincinnati famous. The "resurrection men" would sometimes waylay a stranger in an alley or follow a weaving drunk down a dark street. Once these unlucky victims were dispatched, the corpses were sold to a number of clients in the city's medical schools. If a fresh body was not immediately at hand (or murder was a reluctant enterprise), the body-snatchers could get one that was still reasonably so by waiting for nightfall after a funeral service. Then they would creep into a cemetery, dig up the grave, and retrieve their booty.

The sub-title of this book, "The Queen City Underground," certainly refers to such nefarious activities as grave robbing. But in the main, it points to not only the aspect of the expired life, but to our approach to mourning and the caring treatment of the deceased.

Other than the few pioneer cemeteries that began when Cincinnati was settled in 1788, most of the city's burying grounds had their origins in the mid-1800s. With a population that spread beyond the city's basin by the Ohio River to the hilltop suburbs and the industrialized valleys, Cincinnati's citizens looked for an appropriate locale for their final goodbyes. Spring Grove Cemetery, for instance, was one of the earliest garden cemeteries in the United States. It featured elaborate Victorian monuments that gave symbolic recognition to the "needs" of the dead. Elaborate ponds and gardens define the cemetery grounds, and there are a multitude of human stories that go with the dead found there. An unexpected one, perhaps, is the annual Memorial Day visit by gypsies, who make a pilgrimage to celebrate their ancestors buried there. The gypsies' visit has become a part of Cincinnati legend and is usually accompanied by media warnings about transient flim-flam men.

Other area cemeteries may be less ornate than Spring Grove in their entirety, but there are beautiful monuments nevertheless, and these tombstones have the same architectural function of marking the final journey from the corporeal existence to the spiritual realm.

Chapter one is a look at the culture of death and dying in the city, the disease, health advances, and funeral customs that have grown in Cincinnati, from sickness and health to murders and embalming.

Chapter two is about Spring Grove, one of the loveliest cemeteries in the world. In its accommodation of the dead, it is a vital part of our history, and as an arboretum, as well as a burying ground, Spring Grove is a pastoral treasure.

The third chapter illustrates numerous other cemeteries in the Cincinnati area with their extraordinary monuments and fascinating tales.

And finally, the last chapter, "Our Dearly Departed: Cincinnatians Worth Knowing," puts faces and stories to monuments throughout the city. The individuals included in this chapter are not necessarily the most famous, the most accomplished, the richest, or the most important, but in some way they have had an effect on Cincinnati culture in the broad sense. They are brewers, teachers, musicians, politicians, philanthropists, saints, and sinners. In their times, they were serious, sober, fun, and scandalous—and everything in between. They are part of a heritage that is reflected in everyday life.

In visually telling the tales of Cincinnati cemeteries, our guide is the sentiment expressed by William Makepeace Thackeray in his 1844 novel, *Barry Lyndon*: ". . . good or bad, handsome or ugly, rich or poor, they are all equal now."

Memento Mori.

One

REACHING THE END
OF THE LINE
DEATH AND DYING IN CINCINNATI

The tomb of William Stanley in Spring Grove Cemetery marks one of the earliest styles of stone markers in Cincinnati graveyards. The slab atop the six pedestals is carved with the memorial of Stanley, who was born in Connecticut in 1766, came to Cincinnati in 1790 just two years after the city's founding, fought in the War of 1812 as a major, and died in 1814.

CURE OF CHOLERA.

Fellow Citizens,

Would you be cured of *Cholera* take the disease in time.

It begins with some sort of *Bowel Complaint, or disturbance of the stomach.* In this stage it is easily cured; and all who neglect this stage are in danger of perishing.

Whoever has a *lax* or *sickness* at stomach, or *Colic,* should instantly *take to his bed, in a warm room and drink hot tea of sage, balm, or Thorough wort, or even hot water—bathing his feet if cold, and applying a warm poultice over the bowels.*

Without this nothing will do any good—All who go about in the damp air after the bowel complaint has set in will get Cramps and Spasms and die—I again say they will die!

Besides what I have mentioned, they should take a powder, of ten grains of Calomel and one of Opium mixed, if grown persons, and children should take less in proportion; or a teaspoonful of powdered Rhubarb.

They should, also, take a tea-spoonful, every hour, of the Aromatic Camphorated water, which is a cheap article, and may be had of most of the Apothecaries.

All who are of a full habit, or have Fever, or Colic should be bled.

Again let me warn every one, that the dreadful Epidemic commences as a mild bowel complaint, and in that stage may be cured—when *vomiting coldness* and *spasms* combined, come on, death will follow—has followed, in almost every case that has yet occurred in the city. He who goes about with a mild complaint upon him should expect to perish.

The Epidemic would loose all its terrors, if people would attend, instantly, to the first symptoms—Go to bed, drink hot water or tea, promote a perspiration, and send for their family Physician.

Terror is a great exciting cause. The disease produced by terror requires treatment. Let no one presume to laugh another out of his fears. All the terrified should take to their beds—this will best counteract its bad effects.

Let all who read what is here written, recount it to their friends. Let us unite in aiding each other, for a few days—the Pestilential Cloud will soon pass away. The disease, absolutely, is *not catching*.

Daniel Drake. M. D.

Cincinnati, Saturday afternoon, October, 13th—1832.

Ever concerned for public health, Daniel Drake had a public notice issued during the 1832 cholera epidemic that raged in the city. The notice tells of the symptoms and treatment. That year, Drake also published his study on the disease, detailing its history, prevention, and treatment, for both physicians and the general public. Cholera often took its toll in 19th-century Cincinnati, with serious outbreaks in 1849, 1850, 1866, and 1873. The '49 epidemic was particularly devastating. Hundreds perished, and graveyards were filled with the dead. Fires of tar were set in the streets in the belief the smoke would prevent the spread of the disease. In a touch of the macabre, it is said that a recently named hospital superintendent was named Absalom Death. Decades after, as new cemeteries were created and bodies removed from old ones so families could have their dead near more recently departed relatives, the cholera dead were left untouched for fear of setting off another epidemic.

*"The body-snatchers, they have come,
And made a snatch at me.
It's very hard them kind of men
Won't let a body be!"*

This verse by English poet Thomas Hood illustrates the role of grave robbers in the 19th century. With more than a dozen medical schools in the city, Cincinnati had a great need for fresh bodies for anatomy classes. Stealing into graveyards under cover of darkness, the "sack 'em up men" would dig into a grave at the head of the casket, break through it, and working a rope around the head and shoulders, would haul up the corpse to peddle it to the medical schools. One of the most notorious was William Cunningham, "the Old Dead Man," who would sell bodies for $30 and even shipped them to anatomists in other cities.

With the easing of the laws concerning the use of cadavers for medical education, more anatomy classes had the opportunity to expand their knowledge of life and death. Cincinnati was one of the few cities to offer physician training for women. The top image is of a gross anatomy class at the Laura Memorial Women's Medical College in 1895. The bottom photograph is of medical students at Cincinnati's Ohio Medical College in the 1870s. The passage of the Ohio Anatomy Act in 1881 for the most part ended the illicit practice of corpse-stealing for the medical school dissection classes. A significant cottage industry in Cincinnati was coming to an end.

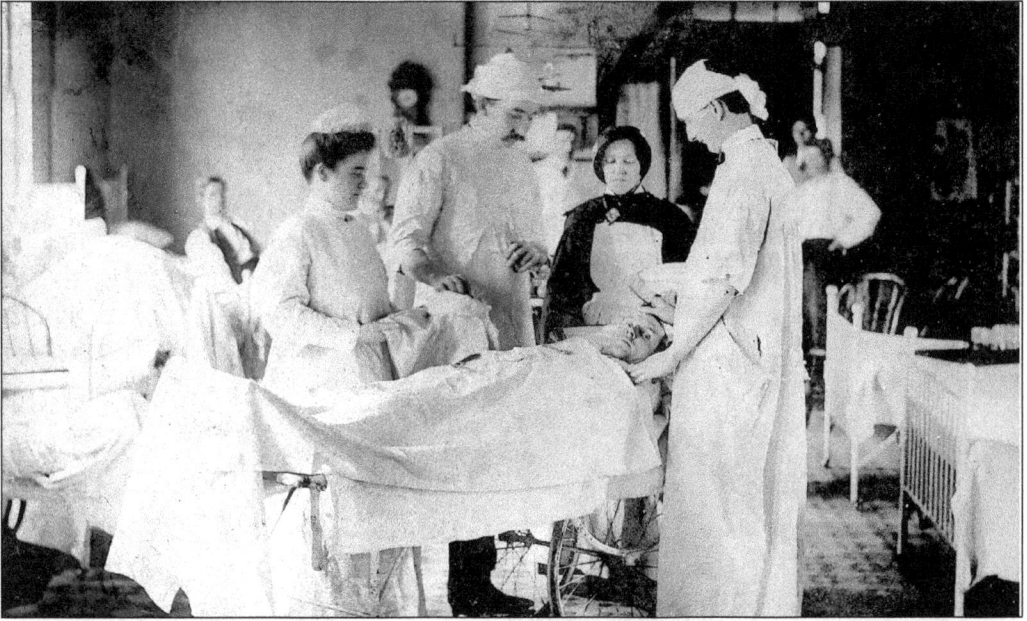

General medical treatment improved in the city as well. With the influence of Daniel Drake's creation of teaching hospitals and new advances in the awareness of germs and infection of patients, the sick and injured had more reason to expect they could stave off that last ride. Any short holiday that Death could take would be a welcome one. One of the innovators in patient care in Cincinnati in the early 20th century was Christian Holmes. He spearheaded the building of a new General Hospital up the hill from downtown. Holmes' plan involved the creation of open pavilions with covered walkways to allow the fresh air and light in, which had been missing from the older dark, stuffy wards.

Violent crimes were part of the burgeoning urban life in early Cincinnati. One of the most horrendous was the murder of Pearl Bryan in 1896. She allegedly came to Cincinnati to tell her lover, Scott Jackson, that she was pregnant. Jackson convinced his friend and fellow dental student, Alonzo Walling, to help him murder Pearl. Tried and convicted, this photograph is of their hanging in Newport, Kentucky, not far from where they dumped her body. Pearl's head was never found.

Modern embalming practices to preserve the dead until burial really began during the Civil War when Thomas Holmes embalmed Union soldiers for shipment home. By the late 19th century, embalming was becoming more of a science, and combined with the funeral business, the undertaker was no longer referred to as "the dismal trader." In Cincinnati, the city's first school of embalming was founded in 1882 by Joseph Henry Clarke, who also wrote a textbook on the topic that same year. This photograph is one of Clarke's early groups of students.

14

JOHN P. EPPLY,
UNDERTAKER,
METALLIC  CASES,
CASKETS AND AIR-TIGHT ZINC CASES,

Wood Coffins, covered with black and white cloth; Black and White Velvet, Satin, Merino, and Luster, &c.; Fine Rosewood and Mahogany finish and Walnut Coffins, ornamented or plain ; Fine Black Cloth, Velvet, Satin, Merino, Silk and Wool Flannel, Luster, Brilliant and Cambric Robes and Shrouds; Hosiery, Gloves, Neck Ties, Cravats and Laces; French, English, and American Crape, Mourning Goods, Ribbons, &c.; Name Plates, Handles, Screw Plates and Screws, Silver Tacks and Ornaments.   **I AM ALSO THE ONLY AGENT FOR THE CITY FOR**

SHOLL'S NEWLY INVENTED PATENT

TERRA COTTA
That will neither

BURIAL CASE,
Rust or decay.

FINE GLASS HEARSES AND CARRIAGES OF THE LATEST STYLES.

MANUFACTORY and STABLES, Nos. 182 and 184 NINTH STREET,
OFFICE, COR. NINTH AND PLUM STS., RESIDENCE, 326 PLUM ST.,
CINCINNATI, OHIO.

N. B.   City and Country Undertakers supplied as usual, on call.

John P. Epply arrived in Cincinnati in 1837 and initially followed the carpenter's trade. In 1848, he was hired by the undertaking firm of P. Rust & Son, but soon after left to start his own company. Epply made a name for himself in 1858 by constructing "glass" hearses, the first used in the United States. He popularized the use of metallic burial cases and expanded his business to include a complete line of undertaker's supplies from casket hardware to clothing with which to attire the deceased. His air-tight zinc burial case presented a tremendous leap forward in corpse-preservation technology. It offered protection from the ravages of the grave and also presented a greater challenge to grave robbers. To discourage "resurrectionists," these metal caskets could be ordered with locking lids. A Columbus firm introduced a much more radical deterrent called a "torpedo" coffin, which contained an explosive device that would detonate if disturbed.

The Cincinnati Coffin Company plant was located at the northeast corner of Richmond and Carr Streets. Founded around 1875, it soon became one of the largest suppliers of coffins and undertaker's supplies in this area. At the end of World War II, the government needed approximately a quarter million memorial caskets to repatriate servicemen lost in battles overseas. CCC was awarded the contract and by updating production methods, was able to produce a repatriation casket every two minutes, a pace maintained until the order was filled.

The Cincinnati Coffin Company was a prolific advertiser, a practice that seems unusual for a casket manufacturer today. However, during the second half of the 19th century, Cincinnati was home to five such firms. It was a competitive market and one in which advertising could determine a company's success. This white-metal disk about the size of a silver dollar is a postage stamp holder. The two halves unscrew to reveal a hollow interior where stamps could be placed and carried until needed.

In 1853, Martin Crane and Abel Breed went into business together to manufacture cast-iron burial cases and hearses. Located on West Eighth Street in Queensgate, the Crane and Breed Casket Company was the first to introduce a shoulder-type zinc casket in 1857. In 1862, the company introduced a rectangular box-shaped casket, which was chosen for President Lincoln's burial in 1865. One of Crane and Breed's horse-drawn hearses won a gold medal at the St. Louis World's Fair in 1904. Two year's later they built the nation's first automobile hearse on a chassis supplied by the Winton Motor Car Company of Cleveland. The company survived nearly 125 years. In January 1977, the old factory was purchased by the Postal Employees Credit Union and demolished later that year.

MEMORIAL SERVICES

IN HONOR OF

Mr. Reuben R. Springer

——MUSIC HALL,——

SUNDAY, JANUARY 11, 1885,

2.30 p. m.

Public memorial services for departed civic leaders were frequent occurrences during the late 19th and early 20th centuries. This service for Reuben R. Springer was held in Music Hall, the building his generosity helped construct. Memorial booklets, containing biographical information and transcripts of the speeches made in honor of the deceased, can still be found occasionally in used bookstores and antique shops.

IN LOVING REMEMBRANCE OF

Minerva V. Beane,
Born July 29, 1871.
Died June 30, 1909.
Age 37 yrs. 11 mos. 1 day.

Gone but not forgotten

We weep for her, no tenderer wife
E'er made man's fireside bright.
No more devoted mother love
E'er kept home altar fires alight.
And she is with the angel host
With sinless heart and stainless hand,
Waiting to meet the friends to come,
To that bright and happy land.

Copyright 1904 by H. F. Wendell & Co., Leipsic, O.

This memorial card marks the passing of Minerva V. Beane, aged 37 years, 11 months, and 1 day. These remembrances were extremely popular around the turn of the last century and were produced by the thousands. This example from a local estate was made by the H.F. Wendell & Co. of Leipsic, Ohio.

Located at 525 Martin Luther King Jr. Drive, the Cincinnati Cremation Company was organized in October of 1884 by a group of far-sighted Cincinnatians concerned about the social, health, and environmental issues associated with traditional ground burial. The original building was erected in 1888 on a hilltop overlooking the Mill Creek Valley in Clifton Heights. It is the oldest operating crematory in the United States.

This *circa* 1900 image shows the "retorts" used for incineration. Fueled by natural gas and operating at 1,800 degrees, each can reduce an adult corpse to one to four pounds of ashes in about two hours. Bodies are prepared in the same manner as for interment and the corpse and casket are placed inside and consumed together. The fire does not directly contact either, but circulates around the retort, reducing its contents to ashes by the action of the heat only.

Another 1900 vintage interior view, this of the crematory's chapel/columbarium, shows the niches where urns containing cremation remains were placed. A 1941 addition to the original structure provided a new chapel and two new columbaria, the "Hall of Peace" and the "Chapel of Light."

Perhaps a bit overdressed, this *circa* 1938 hearse would have lent a macabre elegance to any funeral procession. Victorian-style ruched draperies shield the coffin bay from curious onlookers. The side-panel coach lights and gothic window trim would delight the Munster family of 1960s sitcom fame. The overall design of the vehicle certainly leaves no doubt as to its purpose.

Little seems to have changed in funeral home furnishings since this photograph was taken in the 1920s—with the possible exception of more comfortable seating. Seen here is the beautiful chapel at the Busse & Borgmann funeral home on Central Parkway.

Two

BEAUTY AND
REMEMBRANCE
SPRING GROVE CEMETERY

Spring Grove Cemetery was created in 1845 as a result of the several epidemics of cholera that swept the city. The intent was to create a garden-like park that dignified death through proper interment and provided a pastoral setting for the bereaved. This early postcard view shows one of the lakes and the monuments that border it.

CERTIFICATE OF OWNERSHIP.

The Proprietors of the **Cemetery of Spring Grove,** hereby certify that Thomas J. Henderson, Maria A. Van Matre, John C. Henderson, Ellen G. Nimmo & Mary A. Gajani are the owners of lot No. **182** in Section **31** on the Plat of said Cemetery Grounds, in the County of Hamilton & State of Ohio, containing **321** square feet, for which said Henderson, Van Matre, Henderson, Nimmo & Gajani have paid the sum of **80 & 25/100** dollars, and the said Henderson, Van Matre, Henderson, Nimmo & Gajani, their heirs and assigns are entitled to the use of said lot in fee simple for the purpose of sepulture alone, subject to the provisions of the Charter passed at the forty third session of the General Assembly of Ohio, January 21st 1845. Entitled "An Act to incorporate the Proprietors of the Cemetery of Spring Grove."

In Testimony whereof the said Proprietors of the Cemetery of Spring Grove have caused these presents to be signed by their President and Countersigned by their Secretary, and their Corporate Seal to be hereunto affixed this **21st** day of **Sept**, in the year of our Lord one thousand eight hundred and **sixty, 1860,**

R. Buchanan President

Cyrus Davenport, Secretary.

This certificate of ownership for a plot in section 31 of the Cemetery of Spring Grove is dated September 21, 1860. Signed by Robert Buchanan, one of the founders of Spring Grove and its first president, it contains a vignette of the original entrance to the grounds. Complaints that these structures lacked dignity led to their replacement later in the decade.

This Norman Gothic administration building and a matching gatehouse were completed in 1867 to replace the frame structures that originally marked the entrance to Spring Grove. Both of these new structures were designed by noted Cincinnati architect, James Keys Wilson. The lead vehicles in an approaching funeral procession have been captured in this image. Note the horse-drawn glass hearse followed by carriages of mourners.

The lawn plan of the cemetery provided an elegant setting for the figurative monuments that marked the graves of Cincinnati's prominent citizens. The grounds also conveyed a tranquil, rural setting that some days would attract dozens of people who quietly strolled the grounds.

No. 712. Lake in Spring Grove Cemetery, Cincinnati.

Adolph Strauch was hired as Spring Grove's landscape gardener in October 1854 and was promoted to cemetery superintendent by 1859. Strauch transformed the swampy lowlands at the front of the cemetery into scenic lakes, one of which is seen in this postcard image.

12. - CINCINNATI (Ohio). - Spring Grove Cemetery

Young & Carl, phot.   Handcolored

The rural nature of the area is apparent in this *circa* 1910 postcard image of the administration building at Spring Grove's main entrance.

Spring Grove Cemetery was just down the road from Chester Park, a popular amusement park in the late 19th and early 20th centuries. The Winton Place station on the Baltimore & Ohio rail line was the point Cincinnatians debarked for an afternoon of swimming, rides, and concerts at Chester Park. Bicyclists also traveled along Spring Grove Avenue between the cemetery and the park, but they were forbidden from using the cemetery's roadways because of the wagons and strolling pedestrians there.

The stone water tower in the northern area of Spring Grove is a functioning reservoir, created by cemetery superintendent William Salway in the 1880s. During his tenure, after Strauch's death in 1883, the English-born Salway expanded the landscaping of Spring Grove into new areas and recognized that function had to support design. The structure stands 143 feet above the lakes and draws its water supply from wells dug down into natural springs.

Adolf Strauch and William Salway spent decades sculpting the lakes into Spring Grove's design. Their intent was to create a series of irregular lakes and peninsulas that would echo the curves and depths of the cemetery plots.

Born in Devonshire, England, in 1835, Samuel Hannaford came to Cincinnati and established what became the city's most prominent architectural firm. Hannaford designed Music Hall, City Hall, and other notable public and private buildings and residences. His contribution to Spring Grove Cemetery is the magnificent Mortuary Chapel seen in the photograph below. Built in 1879–1880 and constructed of rough-hewn limestone and sandstone, its relatively plain exterior is accented by the occasional gargoyle. Once inside the visitor is treated to intricately-patterned arches and pillars of Bedford limestone and stained-glass windows designed by Thomas Noble, then head of Cincinnati's Art Academy. The massive bronze doors contain bas relief panels depicting Biblical scenes. The structure also has transepts for use as a temporary receiving tomb, although it was never used for that purpose.

An 1869 history of the cemetery referred to it as an "ornamental burial ground," and in that sense, Spring Grove has always functioned as sort of a museum without walls for the city by commemorating the people that built Cincinnati. The publication is not only a history of the short life of Spring Grove at that time, but a guide to what constitutes a beautiful rural cemetery: it "should exhibit, in its classical purity, a just medium between too great simplicity and the excessive ornament usually met with."

Now called the White Pine Chapel, this building was originally designated the Receiving Tomb. It was built in 1852 by engineer John Earnshaw to hold bodies temporarily in the winter when the ground was too frozen for digging graves. By 1880, as many as 200 bodies could be held there. Sometimes bodies were placed there for a brief time to thwart the "resurrectionists." Cedar shelving had to be installed in 1872 to offset the odors of decaying bodies.

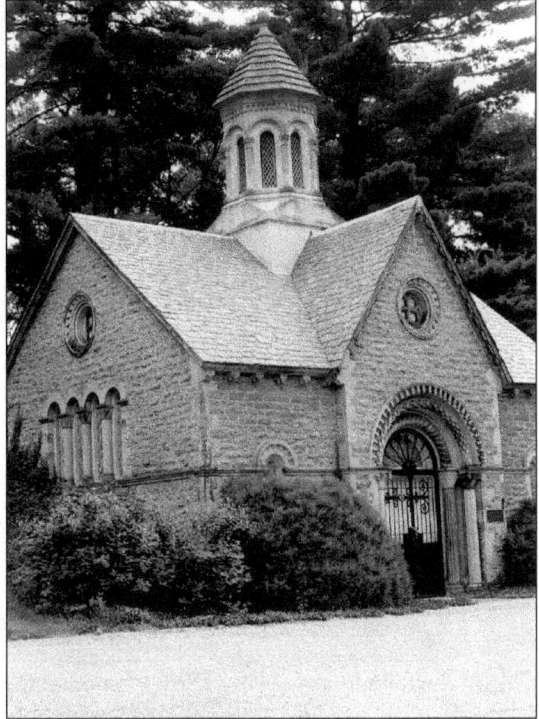

In the winter of 1937, Cincinnati endured its most devastating flood ever when melting snows and torrential rains combined to inundate the city. The Ohio River crested at 80 feet, and the Mill Creek, just to the east of the cemetery, flooded Spring Grove Avenue and the surrounding neighborhoods. The Norman Chapel had to be restored, but there was a curious benefit: the silt and dead fish that accumulated on the cemetery grounds served to enrich the soil.

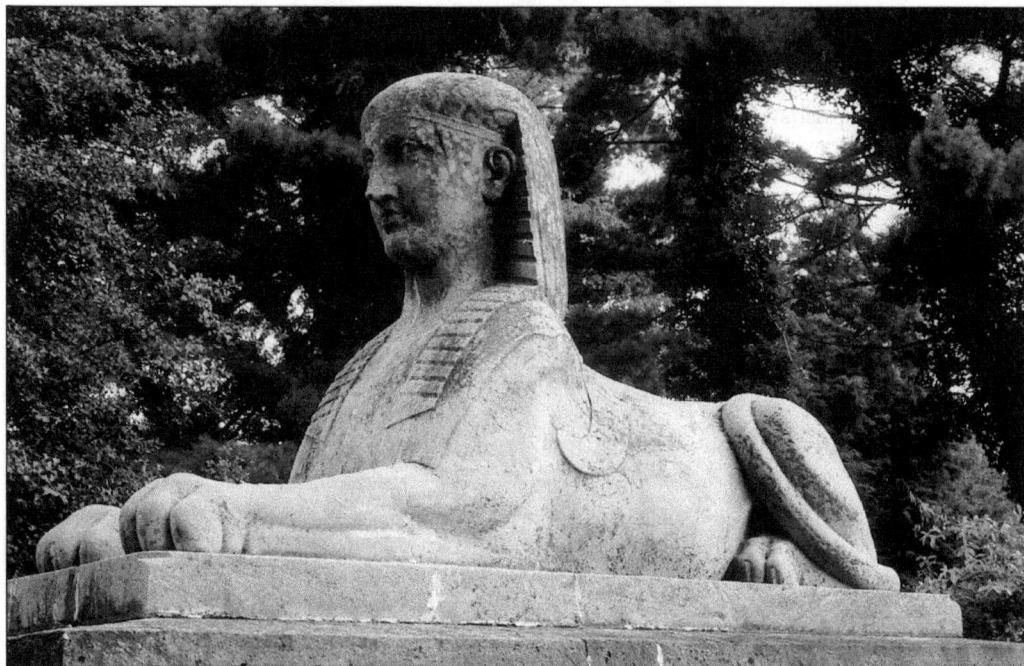

One of the founders of Spring Grove, David Lawler, installed a controversial monument in 1850 when he used the figure of the Sphinx on his family plot. Carved in bluestone on a granite base, the Sphinx was noted with some comment that it was anti-Christian. However, in a cemetery with the Egyptian influence already exhibited through obelisks, and classical influence evident through Greek-styled columns, it was perfectly appropriate. Lawler died in 1869 and is buried there with his parents, brothers, and wife.

The Egyptian motif continues in Spring Grove with the monument on the graves of William N. Groff and his wife, Sarah Talbot Groff. William Groff was a physician who was also involved in classical studies. He belonged to the Asiatic Society and the Egyptian Institute, so he chose a pyramid to mark his final resting place. Sarah Groff died in Egypt in 1900, and her husband died in Athens the following year.

The allegorical statuary of Spring Grove creates a bridge between the natural world and what people expect of the next. On one tomb, a mourning figure holding an anchor symbolizes hope. On the Ringgold tomb, erected in 1865, the Angel of the Resurrection holds a trumpet, ready to signal the approach of Judgment Day. Angel figures in general symbolize many things: mercy, love, protection, and resurrection.

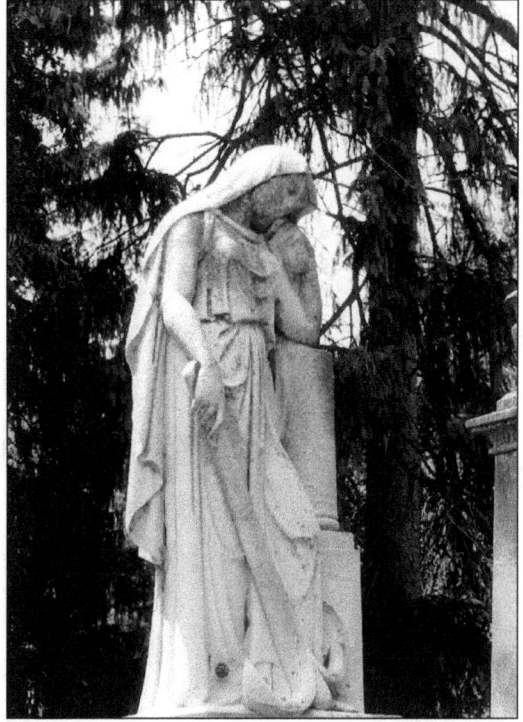

The top image is of the mausoleum for the Strader family. Jacob Strader was a wealthy steamboat trader and railroad tycoon in 19th-century Cincinnati. His Gothic brown sandstone tomb was built in 1858 and has space for 26 catacombs. The bottom photograph is of Judge Jacob Burnet's mausoleum. Burnet, who died in 1853, was one of Cincinnati's earliest settlers, arriving in the city in 1796. His tomb was designed by a local architect, Charles Rule, and built along Cedar Lake in 1865. Though it incorporates several styles, Baroque, French Second Empire, and Corinthian, they come together harmoniously.

The magnificent miniature of Paris' Sainte-Chapelle is the Dexter Mausoleum, designed by James Keys Wilson for Cincinnati's Dexter brothers. In 1842, the influential Edmond Dexter had hosted Charles Dickens at his home at Fourth and Broadway. The Dexters wanted to erect their mausoleum here, but this site had been previously chosen by superintendent Strauch for his family's use. Eventually, the cemetery board settled the dispute by giving Strauch the island in Geyser Lake, which today bears his name. Joseph Foster of Cincinnati built the ornate gothic structure in 1865–1869 at a cost of $100,000. The marble interior contains a vault with 12 catacombs on the lower level and a chapel above. An earlier covering of English ivy contributed to the decay of the brown sandstone exterior. This, combined with structural problems, has made the beautiful structure problematic for the cemetery to maintain.

There is a subdued, serene beauty to most of the figurative sculptures in Spring Grove. The eyes of the statues are often downcast in a quiet splendor, and the languid cast of the faces conveys the cultural sense that peace is an expected aspect of the afterlife. The two images on this page of funerary faces exhibit this facet of the monuments.

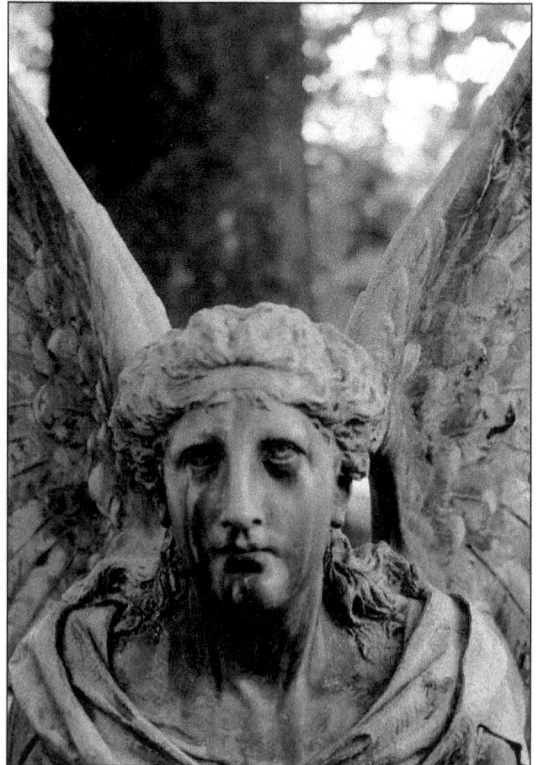

This photograph is a bronze, kneeling angel, hidden away in a shady glen. Its beautiful green patina gives it an uncommon elegance, and below it is written this sentiment: "May this memorial to Sheldon and Albert Thomas Emery gather many into Christ's love."

The first above-ground tombs, or mausoleums, appeared during the tenure of Adolph Strauch as superintendent and landscape architect. Strauch believed the mausoleums should enhance the surrounding landscape by being integrated into its design.

This mausoleum, shown from the rear with its stained glass windows, blends into the trees of the lot on which it is situated. The top photograph of the Rodman mausoleum shows the Gothic Revival tomb designed by New York architect H.O. French, a miniature church with an "aedicule" form, or opened-framed shape.

The symbol of the pointing finger, seen in the statue of the angel atop the Gall monument and as a solitary hand on the Brockman-Phiester stone, indicate the sentiment of "going home," pointing heavenward to eternal salvation. The Gall angel also holds a symbolic representation of the book of life, on which one's deeds and transgressions have been recorded.

A statue of Egeria, the Roman goddess associated with water and with childbirth, stands at the edge of Strauch Island by Geyser Lake. Egeria was sculpted by Nathan Foster Baker, who worked in Florence from 1841 to 1850. Taking his inspiration from a poem by Lord Byron, "Childe Harold's Pilgrimage," Baker's goddess gave "the purity of Heaven to earthly joys." Baker's figure was exhibited in 1847 at both the National Academy and at the Boston Athenaeum. Now gazing down at a lake bordered by cypress knees and swans, Egeria was purchased by a man named Walter Gregory and given to Adolf Strauch and the cemetery. Supposedly it was one of the first statues installed at Spring Grove that was not intended to mark a grave, but simply to add classical beauty to a bucolic setting.

She died of scarlet fever on March 28, 1884, at the age of three, and her monument commemorates her as "Chunkie" Singleton. The Singleton family lived in Covington, Kentucky, across the Ohio River from Cincinnati, and the girl's death must have been devastating to them. Her life-sized marble statues shown here dressed in pinafore and bonnet, holding an umbrella in her right hand, and her epitaph says, "Only God knows how we miss her."

The Edwards monument is one of the more unusual ones in the cemetery. Sculpted of marble, a mermaid stands beneath a classical portal. At first glance, the statue looks like so many other female figures, but the lower torso is that of a fish, and dolphins swim about her feet. Called *Origin of the Harp*, the seven-foot statue was sculpted by Louis Lawson in Rome in 1887 and displayed at Music Hall in 1893. Sometime in the mid-20th century the sculpture was placed on the Edwards tomb, but the reason is unknown. Ironically, Edward Edwards (1874–1956) manufactured caskets and burial vaults as part of his building material business.

In the image on the right, a mourning woman, elegantly carved in marble, is symbolic of the sorrow felt by those left behind. The wreath she holds signifies the victory of salvation and the joy to be found in heaven. The bottom photograph shows the grimacing faces of death at the bottom of a large urn, symbolizing the return of the body to dust in its final earthly resting place.

Contributing to the beauty of the monuments in Spring Grove Cemetery is the diversity of form. Though the 19th-century funerary architecture is laden with classical elements, the variety of height and placement still contribute to the landscape. The forms also reflect the aesthetics of a particular era. More modern expressions of aesthetic design can be seen in the polished granite sphere and the balanced cube of these two graves.

Modern design in conjunction with traditional gravestone shapes continues with the carved harp on the Smith plot and the stainless steel cross on S.B. Thomson's grave. The cross' wreath of polished stainless steel adds a brilliantly reflected aspect to the monument.

A bronze statue of Johnny Appleseed dominates the landscape at the northern end of the cemetery. Created by artist Robert Koepnick, the representation of the legendary side of missionary John Chapman shows him scattering apple seeds to the wind to symbolize the spirit of giving and of faith. The statue was erected in 1968.

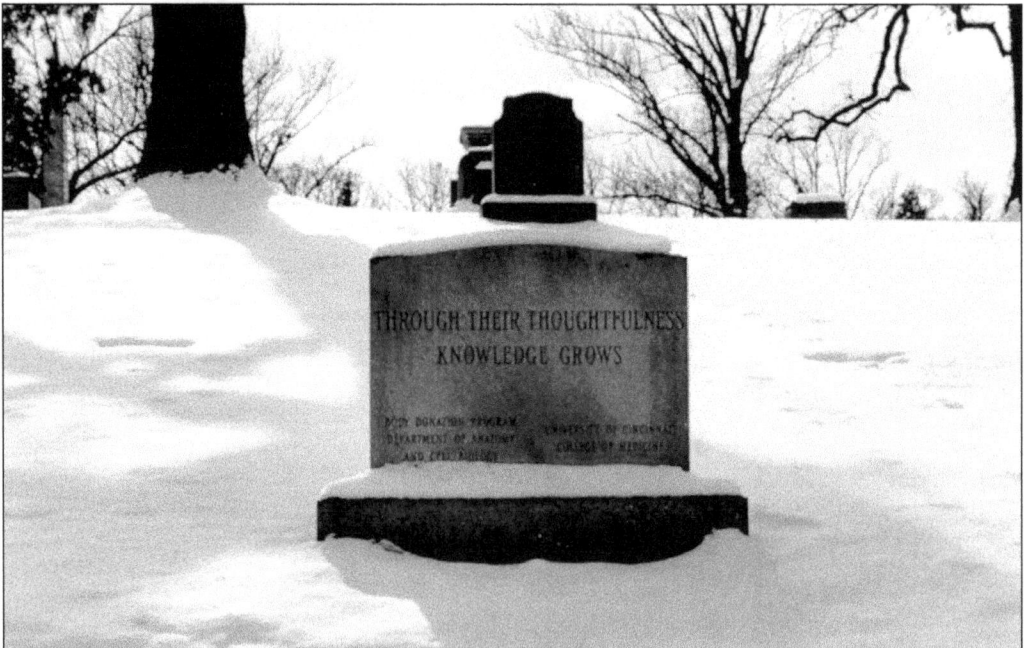

There are no single names on this monument, but the marker commemorates the gifts of hundreds of people. "Through their thoughtfulness, knowledge grows" is the inscription that acknowledges those people who donated their bodies to the University of Cincinnati College of Medicine in the cause of education. Nestled in the side of a hill, the marker also serves as an acknowledgment of the ultimate ties between individuals and their community.

Three

TESTAMENTS OF TIME
NOTABLE CEMETERIES
AND MONUMENTS

The United American Cemetery on Duck Creek Road near Strathmore Drive is the oldest African-American cemetery in Ohio. It was founded in 1844 by the United Colored American Association and was dedicated in 1847. Buried here are John Isom Gaines, an early educator and advocate of free public education for African-American children, and Horace Sudduth (1898–1957), proprietor of the Manse Hotel in Walnut Hills and a real estate speculator and financier. Sudduth owned the Industrial Federal Savings & Loan, later known as Charter Oak Savings, and through this institution provided mortgage loans to hundreds of African Americans.

The cholera epidemic of 1849–1854 devastated the Catholic immigrant population of Cincinnati's basin and West End, causing the original St. Joseph Cemetery to quickly reach its capacity. The situation was so dire that cholera victims were buried one on top of the other, and Delhi Township farmers taking produce to town were often required to haul bodies to St. Joseph's on their return trip home. In 1853, Archbishop Purcell bought just over 61 acres of farm land approximately two miles west of the original location and established the New St. Joseph Cemetery. Over the years, the cemetery has grown to 163 acres and even acquired a small Protestant cemetery in the process. Located along Covedale Avenue, this tiny "cemetery within a cemetery" was the site of the Delphi Universalist Church from 1838–1872. The 29 graves on this one-half acre of land are maintained by the St. Joseph Cemetery Association. In 1964, a new administration building was dedicated along with the 43-foot bell tower seen here. Located near the intersection of Pedretti and Foley Roads, the facility provided much needed office space and an interment chapel where services can be held during inclement weather.

This huge mausoleum is located near Nebraska Avenue, not far from the original entrance to New St. Joseph Cemetery at the end of West Eighth Street. It was opened in 1911, contains 1,200 crypts, and is believed to be the fourth largest public mausoleum in the United States. The exterior is constructed of limestone and granite and the interior of imported Carrara marble. Natural lighting is supplied to the interior by 51 stained and leaded glass windows. The building was completely refurbished in 1990 at a cost of $650,000.

One of the most beautiful mausoleums in Cincinnati cemeteries is the O'Brien tomb in New St. Joseph's Cemetery. Reportedly costing $75,000 at its construction in 1925, a figure that would exceed $2 million if it was built today, the tomb contains a full chapel with stained glass windows, marble statues of saints, gold architectural details, and fabulous mosaics. Very little is known of the two bachelor O'Brien brothers, Robert and John, who are buried there, except that they were known for their kindness to orphans and that they donated the undercroft to the Little Sisters of the Poor for indigent burials in the 21 crypts located there.

John Keating was a stonemason devoted to his daughters and his niece. Sadly, all three girls died in the decade between 1868 and 1878, and a distraught Keating resolved to commemorate their young lives by carving a doll house for their graves in New St. Joseph's Cemetery in Price Hill. Supposedly the house, whose interior can be seen by peering through the windows, at one time contained doll furniture. The inscription on the marker reads: "One by one the leaves are falling, fading day by day. And in silence heaven is calling, one by one our lambs away."

The 1906 gravestone of Patrick McAvoy in New St. Joseph's Cemetery tells the story of the signature moment of his life. McAvoy worked at the Cincinnati Zoo, and one day in September 1875, a lioness escaped from her cage. The escape occurred just a few days before the zoo was scheduled to open to the public. The lioness first attacked a donkey and then turned on some workers who tried to capture it. McAvoy grabbed a rifle and shot the lion to save his fellow employees, and it is said that for the rest of his life, he could walk into any bar in the city and be treated to a drink for his heroism. His weathered marker portrays him shooting the lion that stands over a fallen man.

This boulder marks the entrance to the original, or Old St. Joseph Cemetery on West Eighth Street in Price Hill. Archbishop John B. Purcell purchased the land in 1842. He was immediately petitioned by both German and Irish Catholics, each asking that the new burial ground be set aside for the exclusive use of Catholics of their individual ethnic origins. To solve this dilemma, the archbishop divided the land into German Catholic and Irish Catholic sections. As the surrounding city grew, West Eighth Street was extended through the cemetery, and many graves in the Irish section were relocated to the new cemetery. Today, a remnant of the Irish section is still maintained at the northwest corner of West Eighth and Enright. The German inscription on the monument pictured is representative of hundreds of others found here.

Located on Cleves-Warsaw Road on the west side of the city, Union Baptist Cemetery was founded in 1864 and is the oldest African-American denominational cemetery still in use in Cincinnati and Hamilton County. Among the many prominent African-American Cincinnatians buried in this historic cemetery is Powhatan Beaty, who was awarded the Medal of Honor for his courageous service in the Union Army during the Civil War. Beaty was a sergeant in Company C, 5th United States Colored Troops when he assumed command during a battle against Confederate troops at New Market Heights, Virginia, in 1864 after all his officers were killed or wounded. As part of the Underground Railroad Heritage program, a marker commemorates his bravery. Beaty died in 1916; he is joined in the cemetery by more than a hundred other soldiers in the Colored Troops.

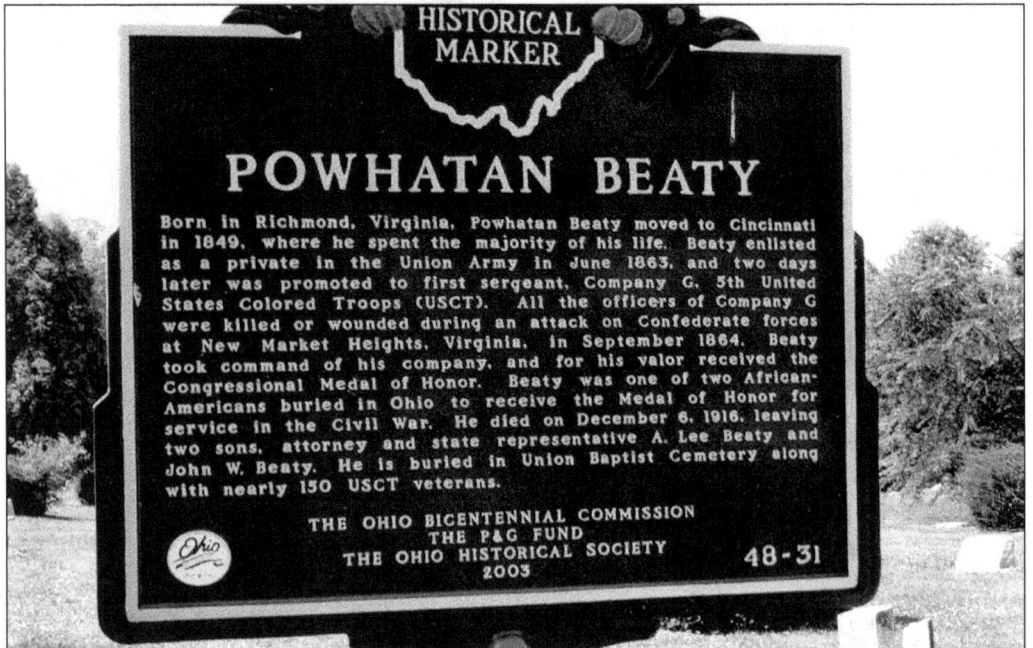

This towering, 60-foot monument of Bedford limestone marks the tomb of William Henry Harrison, ninth president of the United States. It is situated at North Bend, Ohio, on Mt. Nebo, a prominence having a commanding view of a broad curve in the Ohio River. In earlier days, steamboat captains would sound their whistles out of respect for the former president when passing this point. Harrison was born in Berkeley County, Virginia, in 1773. Upon entering the army, he was stationed at Fort Washington in Cincinnati and served as General Anthony Wayne's aide-de-camp during the Indian campaigns. Harrison's impressive military and political career also included appointments as the Secretary of the Northwest Territory, governor of the Indiana Territory, and commander of the Army of the Northwest Territory during the War of 1812. At the end of the war, he was elected to Congress, then to the Senate, and was appointed minister to Columbia in 1828. During the late 1830s, local supporters began the boisterous "log cabin and hard cider" campaign that carried him to the White House. On April 4, 1841, exactly one month after his inauguration, he died of pneumonia. His body was returned to North Bend via steamboat, and a tomb was built at this site. With the passage of time, both the tomb and the nearby Congress Green Cemetery, where many of Harrison's family are buried, suffered from neglect. In 1919, a state bill was introduced, appropriating $10,000 to return the tomb and the surrounding grounds to "a suitable and decent condition." Groundbreaking ceremonies took place on October 24, 1921, and the work was completed during the spring of 1922. The entire area is now the William Henry Harrison State Park and is operated by the Ohio Historical Society.

Soon after John Cleves Symmes and his original band of settlers arrived at North Bend in 1789, he set aside a parcel of land for use as a burial ground. Legend has it that the first person buried here was a soldier who was killed in a brawl at a frontier tavern nearby. Early interments continued, most without permanent markers, and the area became known as the "pasture graveyard." The name "Congress Green" came into use years later and was taken from one of Symmes' early plans for a town square.

The final resting place of John Cleves Symmes (1742–1814) is under this false crypt in Congress Green Cemetery. Symmes purchased the huge tract of land between the two Miami Rivers, which became known as the Miami Purchase. In his zeal to settle the area, he sometimes sold land before having legal title to it. Eventually, most of his personal property had to be sold to settle lawsuits filed over disputed titles. Symmes' daughter, Anna, married William Henry Harrison.

John Scott Harrison (1804–1878) was the youngest son of William Henry Harrison and the father of Benjamin Harrison, the 23rd president. As a congressman from Ohio, he had the dubious honor of being responsible for as much legislation after his death as before. Harrison died on May 26, 1878, and was buried at Congress Green Cemetery three days later. Mourners attending his service noticed that the grave of William B. Devin, a young friend of the Harrisons who had died a few days earlier, had been disturbed, and his body was missing. Due to this gruesome discovery, grave watchers were hired to guard the site. The next day, John Scott Harrison's son John and nephew, George Eaton, began the search for Devin's body. Aided by police, they inspected the premises of the Ohio Medical College on Sixth Street in downtown Cincinnati. They searched in vain and were about to leave when police noticed a doorway leading to a shaft. Inside the shaft, a taut rope held a male body. The men stripped off a sheet covering the head and shoulders expecting to find Devin. Instead they were confronted with the corpse of John Scott Harrison! The court proceedings that followed revealed that the college, in addition to several other medical schools in the area, was under contract to receive bodies for dissection. Cincinnati, it appeared, was the center of a cadaver procurement and shipping operation. (Devin's corpse was later found in Michigan.) John Scott Harrison was re-interred, but newspaper accounts of his postmortem travels drew much attention to the need for legislative change.

Washington Park, Cincinnati, Ohio.

During the first half of the 19th century, the area now occupied by Washington Park had been the Twelfth Street Burying Ground. It received re-interments from many of Cincinnati's older cemeteries as overcrowding and increasing land values in the business core forced their removal. Unfortunately, the bodies moved here did not find eternal rest. In 1855, the city purchased this land, and the graves were ordered moved, many for the second time. Most were re-interred in Wesleyan and Spring Grove cemeteries.

Cincinnati's Music Hall stands where the city's first contagious diseases ward and potter's field were located. Later, poor patients who died at the Commercial Hospital & Lunatic Asylum across the canal (now Central Parkway) were buried here. Stories of hauntings were first heard after Saengerfest Hall was built on the site in 1870. But it wasn't until excavating for Music Hall began in 1876 that the first human bones were unearthed. To this day, these bones have not been allowed to rest, and night watchmen tell tales of shadowy figures that accompany them on their appointed rounds.

POTTER'S FIELD

1849

PUBLIC BURIAL PLACE FOR THOSE
WHO HAVE NO ONE TO PROVIDE
FOR THEIR BURIAL

THE ORIGINAL POTTER'S FIELD WAS
BOUGHT WITH THE THIRTY PIECES
OF SILVER WHICH JUDAS WAS PAID
TO BETRAY JESUS. HIS GUILT WAS
SO GREAT, HE HUNG HIMSELF ON A
JUDAS TREE. KNOWN IN OUR COUNTRY
AS A RED-BUD TREE.

DONATED BY
CENTAUR'S 4-H SADDLE CLUB
NOV. 2, 1969

About the time the city was converting the Twelfth Street Burying Ground into Washington Park, the old Potter's Field nearby was also closed to burials. A new cemetery for the poor, unwanted, and unknown was established in 1849 along Guerley Road in rural Price Hill. The history of this cemetery is closely connected to the city-owned hospital that stood where the Dunham Recreation Complex is now located. General Hospital built the facility in 1879 for the treatment of patients with highly contagious diseases such a cholera, typhoid, small pox, and tuberculosis. Although officially designated the "Branch Hospital for Contagious Diseases," it was called the "pest house" by local residents. Any unclaimed body from either facility is likely to have ended up in Potter's Field. After embalming, bodies were placed in pine boxes made by workhouse prisoners and buried quickly, without the customary funeral services. Most burial sites were unmarked although some had metal plates or wooden stakes marking their graves. After the hospital closed in 1912, the Hamilton County Welfare Department took over operation of the cemetery. Between 1849 and May 1981, between 8,500 and 10,000 people were laid to rest on this 25-acre site. Today the only evidence that a cemetery exists here is this plaque, erected in 1969 by the Centaur's 4-H Saddle Club.

Wesleyan Cemetery was chartered in 1843, making it the oldest continuously operating cemetery in Hamilton County. Wesley Chapel was one of the four Methodist churches that joined together to purchase the original 25 acres in rural Cumminsville. When Procter & Gamble expanded their corporate headquarters downtown, the original church building was razed. The burials from this site were re-interred at Wesleyan in 1972. This marker, along with many original gravestones, is dedicated to the memory of those early settlers.

Wesleyan contains many notable burials, including William Steinmetz, who won the Medal of Honor at Vicksburg; Thomas V. Morrow, who founded the Eclectic Medical Institute in Cincinnati in 1845; John Van Zandt, an abolitionist who was immortalized as "John Van Trompe" by Harriet Beecher Stowe; and Fred Waterman, third baseman for the 1869 Cincinnati Red Stockings. Unfortunately, Wesleyan's recent past has been troubled as plot owners and relatives have voiced concerns over conditions at the cemetery.

From 1849–51, David Fisher was a U.S. congressman from Wilmington, Ohio, who later moved to Cincinnati. Interestingly, Fisher was seated next to former President John Quincy Adams when Adams, in the midst of a speech, collapsed into Fisher's arms. Adams was taken to a nearby corridor in the House chambers where he died.

Perhaps Wesleyan's most famous "resident" is Richard Allison (1757–1816). Allison was a Revolutionary War soldier who was appointed Army Surgeon by the first U.S. Congress. He then served as surgeon general under Arthur St. Clair, Josiah Harmar, and Anthony Wayne. He was also the first physician and surgeon at Ft. Washington and in the City of Cincinnati. His body was moved to Wesleyan, presumably from the Twelfth Street Burying Ground.

Located at 1721 Duck Creek Road in Evanston, Calvary Cemetery was established in 1865 by members of St. Francis de Sales parish in Walnut Hills. When the cemetery was established, the area was mostly farmland. The surrounding wall was built to keep livestock from trampling graves and pushing over monuments.

The first burial was that of an infant, Katherine Hoffstedder, in November 1865. Since that time, more that 17,000 interments have been made. Of interest is the marker of Stephan G. Weaver, which contains the following inscription: "President Lincoln's last guard at the White House."

The Heekin family plot is noteworthy for its orderly appearance. The plot's borders are defined on three sides by white curbing topped by a low chain fence. Anchoring the plot is a huge polished-stone cross. Each individual grave is identified by similarly shaped markers, and many are also defined with curbing, giving them an almost bed-like appearance perhaps symbolic of eternal rest.

By far, the most massive marker in Calvary Cemetery is this one, dedicated to the memory and service of Martin Fox (1848–1907). Fox was president of the International Molders' Union of North America from 1890 to 1903.

The United Jewish Cemetery, 3400 Montgomery Road, was the first burial ground in the vicinity. It was founded in 1850 by two reform Jewish Congregations, Bene Israel (Rockdale Temple) and B'nai Yeshurun (Wise Temple), after the Jewish cemetery on Chestnut Street reached capacity. Many burials pre-dating 1871 were reinterred here from a burial ground next to the Brighton House Hotel in downtown Cincinnati. United Jewish Cemetery is surrounded by a wall, which, like that of the adjacent Calvary Cemetery, was originally built to keep farm animals out of this, at one time, rural cemetery. A Soldiers Monument was erected in 1868 to honor Civil War veterans. Later the names of veterans of World Wars I and II were added. A burial of note is that of David Urban (Urbansky), the first Jewish serviceman to receive the Congressional Medal of Honor.

Located at 3701 Vine Street, the Vine Street Hill Cemetery was founded by members of the German Evangelical Reform Churches of St. Peter and St. Paul. The first land for burial purposes was purchased in 1850. An additional purchase was made in 1882, and the cemetery now contains 170 acres. Burials from the St. Peter Churchyard at 3001 Queen City Avenue were reinterred here in 1871. Originally called the German Evangelical Protestant Cemetery on Carthage Road or simply the Carthage Road Cemetery, the name was changed in 1896 when Cincinnati annexed Clifton and the stretch of Carthage Road running adjacent to the cemetery was renamed Vine Street.

The Walnut Hills Cemetery on Victory Parkway was dedicated as the German Protestant Cemetery in 1843. The first lots were sold in May, and the first burial was made on June 30, 1843. Begun with only five acres of land, there are now 50 acres of beautifully wooded, rolling terrain. The original name was kept despite anti-German sentiment during World War I, but was changed in September 1941 by vote of the cemetery directors. The picturesque stone chapel located in an older section of the cemetery dates from the 1880s.

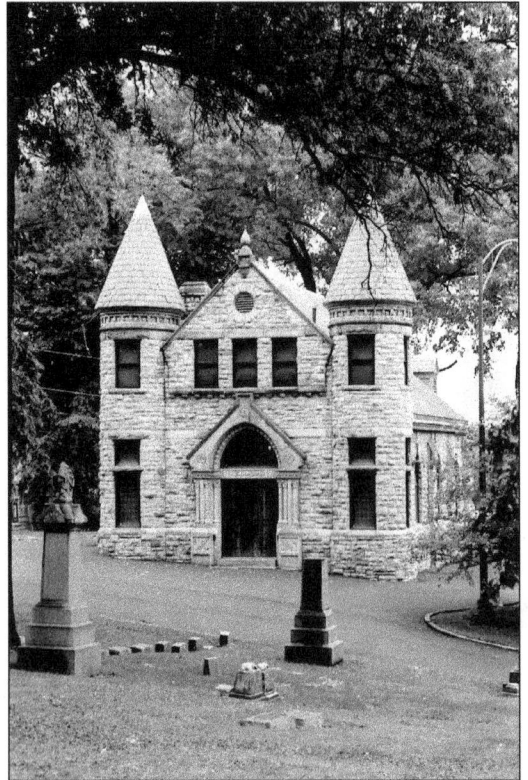

This weathered monument marks the grave of Karl Heizmann (1840–1885). Although the German inscription on the stone is difficult to decipher, the figure of a horse, a horseshoe, and blacksmith tools leave little doubt as to Mr. Heizmann's profession.

Monuments displaying carved busts of the deceased became a popular expression of remembrance in the late 19th century for those families who could afford it. This beautiful monument marks the grave of Johann Georg Sohn (1817–1876), a prosperous Cincinnati brewer. The Sohn Brewery was located on McMicken Avenue in the Mohawk area.

St. Mary Cemetery, located at 701 East Ross Avenue in St. Bernard, had its beginnings in 1873 when the German Catholic Cemetery Society purchased 111 acres of land from the Kemper family. An estimated 15,000 people attended the dedication ceremony at which Archbishop John Purcell performed the blessing. The 1918 flu epidemic necessitated over 1,100 burials at St. Mary's that year, including 23 on a single day, October 28th. The cemetery now averages 400 interments per year. St. Mary's has two mausoleums and a columbarium for cremation remains.

The Abbing family monument memorializes a brother, Anthony Abbing, who was lost on the Titanic. Another commemorates William B. Schmidt, whose submarine was lost in the Pacific during World War II. A notable burial is that of another William Schmidt, who received a Medal of Honor for heroism at the Civil War battle at Missionary Ridge, Tennessee.

In a central section of the cemetery, a crucifix-topped monument stands guard over dozens of tiny headstones. Here are buried children from the St. Aloysius Orphanage who died in the late 1800s.

Laurel Cemetery was established March 27, 1863, by Laurel Lodge No. 191 of the Independent Order of Odd Fellows. The entrance is located at 5915 Roe Street in Madisonville. Originally six acres, it was the first cemetery of size in the area. The surrounding area grew rapidly, and the cemetery received many re-interments from family burial grounds nearby. The cemetery now consists of 13 acres and is within the city limits of Cincinnati.

The small stone building was once a receiving tomb where bodies were held in winter until the ground thawed sufficiently to allow grave digging. The large mausoleum was built in 1929.

Memorial Pioneer Cemetery is located along Wilmer Avenue at Lunken Airport. The Columbia Baptist Church, organized January 30, 1790, was the first Protestant Church established in the Northwest Territory. The cemetery was established in March 1804 and was later transferred to the trustees of the church. Early burials were unmarked or sometimes marked only with a fieldstone. In the mid 1800s, the population of the area continued to shift away from the flood-prone bottomland. The Columbia Baptist congregation moved to a new location, and the cemetery lay forgotten. The city's centennial in 1888 sparked renewed interest in the area's history, and this memorial to the pioneers who settled here in 1788 was erected. The sandstone column was taken from the old Cincinnati Post Office Building that stood on the southwest corner of Fourth and Vine. The cemetery again returned to a neglected state until Edwin Kellogg, a former city councilman, convinced the Baptists to donate the land to the Cincinnati Park Board, which has since been responsible for its upkeep.

Major Benjamin Stites and a group of 26 men, women, and children landed near the mouth of the Little Miami River on November 28, 1788. They built a fort near the Ohio River and farmed the fertile bottomland nearby. Soon the settlers began building homes outside the fort in a town Stites had platted called Columbia. Stites died in 1804 and is buried in Columbia Baptist Cemetery. This marker was erected in 1923 to replace his original, which was lost.

These stones mark the final resting places of the first settlers in this region. Many of these graves are 200 years old.

Mt. Washington Cemetery was established in 1855 by Dove Lodge No. 24 of the Independent Order of Odd Fellows. The lodge purchased 12 acres of land from Stephen Corbly and his wife to be used for school and cemetery purposes. The property was deeded to the Mt. Washington Cemetery Association in 1874. The wrought iron arch over the entrance to the cemetery on Sutton Avenue was given in memory of Herman Becker.

This beautiful fountain is located near the Sutton Avenue entrance to the cemetery. In the background stands a familiar landmark, the Mt. Washington water tower.

These older markers carry the names of the first families to settle in this area. Other notable burials include William "Buck" Ewing, former Cincinnati Reds catcher, and Killian Henry Van Rensselaer, "33rd Degree Mason and former Sovereign Grand Commander of the Scottish Rite in the Northern Mason's Jurisdiction of the U.S., 1861–1867."

This small mortuary chapel was built in 1879 and is located near the center of the cemetery.

Flagspring Cemetery was established in 1863 by Lodge No. 152 of the Independent Order of Odd Fellows. It is located on the west side of Round Bottom Road, just north of Route 32 in Newtown, Anderson Township. The cemetery encircles the largest Adena Indian Mound in the Little Miami Valley (the area covered by trees in the top photograph). The Newtown Methodist Churchyard Cemetery had all burials and markers removed to Flagspring around 1933. In 1952, burials from the Turpin Family Cemetery were moved with their markers to Flagspring. Some of these older gravestones can be seen in the bottom photograph.

Salem Methodist Church, located at the intersection of Salem Road and Sutton Avenue in Mt. Washington, was at the center of a community here named Salem in the early 1800s. Church services were first held in Reverend Francis McCormick's log home. In 1810, a log church was built here on land donated by McCormick for religious and educational purposes. A brick church building followed in 1828. The existing structure was erected in 1863.

The Salem Methodist Cemetery was established in March 1817 by the trustees of the church. The two markers in this photograph are those of Reverend Francis McCormick and his wife Rebecca Easton McCormick. McCormick served in the Revolutionary War and was at the capture of Cornwallis at Yorktown in 1790. He also served in the Ohio State Legislature. McCormick died in 1836 at the age of 72.

Five Mile Chapel was one of the first United Brethren in Christ churches in this area. Jacob Markley donated the land for the church and cemetery. Church members built the chapel with rock from the creek that runs along the front of the property. In 1896, a belfry entrance was added, and the pulpit was moved to the rear of the building. Originally, it had been under the front window, making it easy for the minister to take note of any late arrivals loitering outside. Five Mile Chapel was in continuous use until 1963 when its congregation merged with the Evangelical Brethren Church in Cherry Grove. The unused building and the historic cemetery soon became neglected and fell into disrepair. In 1980, a group of interested citizens formed the Five Mile Chapel Society to restore the building and cemetery. The property was deeded to the Society, funds were raised, and the chapel has now been completely restored.

In 1863, William and Marcia Sibcy donated additional land to expand the tiny cemetery. One of the more interesting monuments here is that of the Markley family. Designed and signed by Cincinnati artist Thomas O'Hare, it includes the faces of three family members sculpted from the stone.

Hillcrest Cemetery is located on the west side of Sutton Avenue about one-quarter mile south of Eversole in Anderson Township. The deed for a burial ground on this site was recorded July 10, 1926, by Guy Lancaster and others who organized under the name of "Hillcrest Cemetery Association." The cemetery covers 14 acres of gently sloping land. The majority of the burials are African-American military veterans.

Four

OUR DEARLY DEPARTED
CINCINNATIANS WORTH KNOWING

Marking the stairs leading to Jacob Hoffner's family tomb at Spring Grove are a pair of lions in repose, one of which is seen here. Hoffner had an affinity for lions: the gardens at his Cumminsville estate also held statues of lions, stone figures that eventually would become part of the landscape at the University of Cincinnati.

CLARA BAUR

Founder of the Cincinnati Conservatory of Music, Clara Baur came to Cincinnati from Germany to visit her brother in the mid 1850s. She soon decided to make Cincinnati her home and to pursue her dream of establishing a music school modeled after the great conservatories of Europe. On December 2, 1867, she opened the first conservatory west of the Alleghenies in rented rooms on West Seventh Street. After surviving the financial panic of 1873, the school moved to a four-story building at the corner of Eighth and Vine Streets. Here, Baur successfully offered boarding to students from out-of-town, a first for any music school in the country. In 1892, the school moved to the former Lytle home at Fourth and Lawrence. Ten years later, the Shillito mansion on Oak Street in Walnut Hills provided an elegant new setting for the conservatory, which later became part of the University of Cincinnati. Miss Clara died December 21, 1912, and is buried in Spring Grove Cemetery.

ENOCH T. CARSON

Born in 1822 in Green Township, Enoch T. Carson made his fortune through real estate speculation and in lamps and gas fixtures. His involvement with Republican politics and his friendship with Cincinnati native and secretary of the Treasury, Salmon Chase, led to his appointment by Abraham Lincoln as collector for the Port of Cincinnati, a position that was of paramount importance during the Civil War when the city was a distributing point for the Union armies in the South. Over his lifetime, he educated himself through reading and travel, amassing a very large Masonic collection and hundreds of volumes of Shakespeare's works. The Shakespearian library became one of the founding collections in the University of Cincinnati libraries in 1899. Carson died in 1899 and is buried in Spring Grove Cemetery.

SALMON P. CHASE

Salmon P. Chase graduated from Dartmouth College in 1826. He was admitted to the bar in December 1829 and moved to Cincinnati. Here he became occupied with anti-slavery activities. Despite scornful opposition, he prominently defended escaping slaves, which earned him the moniker "attorney-general for runaway Negroes." Chase was elected governor of Ohio in 1855 and made several unsuccessful bids for the Republican presidential nomination. He was elected to the Senate in 1860, but resigned to become Secretary of the Treasury. He joined two other Cincinnatians on Lincoln's cabinet: Edwin Stanton (Secretary of War) and William Dennison (Postmaster General). As Treasury Secretary, Chase established the national banking system in 1863. In honor of this achievement, Chase's portrait appears on the $10,000 bill (though the authors have never seen one). In 1864, Lincoln appointed him Chief Justice of the Supreme Court. On April 15, 1865, he administered the presidential oath to Andrew Johnson and later presided over Johnson's impeachment hearings in the Senate. Chase died May 7, 1873, and is buried in Spring Grove Cemetery.

ROBERT CLARKE

When Cincinnati was a major center for book publishing in the 19th century, its most prominent publisher and book dealer was Robert Clarke. Born in Scotland in 1829, Clarke's knowledge of Americana, history, and geography made him an expert in books well beyond those he published. In 1898, a year before Clarke's death, William A. Procter, the second-generation head of the Procter & Gamble Company, purchased the publisher's private library of several thousand volumes and presented them to the University of Cincinnati. Procter was a board member of the university and followed that gift with the Carson Shakespeariana Library, and the chemical library of Thomas Norton. These three collections formed the core of the university's holdings, leading to a collection of more than 3,000,000 volumes today. Buried in Spring Grove Cemetery, Clarke's marker is a modest reflection of a man of considerable learning.

GEORGE BARNSDALE COX

Arguably the most powerful man in Cincinnati politics during the Progressive Era (1880–1920), George Barnsdale Cox was the consummate urban machine boss. Running the Republican Party from behind the scenes at the Mecca saloon, Cox manipulated elections and political offices, always making sure his candidate was in power and then cementing his power through the distribution of patronage jobs. In addition, he was part of the ownership that bought the Cincinnati Reds in 1902, baseball and urban politics always conducive bedfellows. Cox was born in 1853 and grew up on the streets of Cincinnati, wise to how influence was obtained and used. Open to corruption and graft, he was a man who could get things done for powerful Republican leaders like Ohio Governor Joseph Foraker. The ideals of the Progressive Era reformists who sought to eliminate the likes of Cox proved to be his undoing. He resigned leadership of local Republicans in 1911 when reform mayor Henry Hunt was elected. Cox's influence waned, and he died in 1916. He is buried in Spring Grove.

JACOB DOLSON COX

Jacob Dolson Cox (1828–1900) was a general during the Civil War and later served as Ohio's governor from 1866 to 1868. After an appointment as Secretary of the Interior under president Ulysses S. Grant, Cox became head of the Cincinnati College of Law, a school that began in 1833 and merged with the Cincinnati College the next year. While administering the law college, he was named head of the fledgling University of Cincinnati as well, a position he held until 1889. It was under Cox that the university began examining its role as an urban institution. Cox saw higher education as a strong part of service to the larger community, so he brought several independent colleges under the umbrella of UC. The university eventually extended its pedigree back to the 1819 founding of the Cincinnati College when it absorbed the Law School into is own college of law in 1897.

POWEL CROSLEY

For most people, the name "Crosley" brings back memories of Crosley Field, the home of the Cincinnati Reds until 1970. Industrialist and inventor Powel Crosley bought the Reds in 1934, renaming the ballpark called Redland Field after himself. The purchase was a little unexpected for Crosley, but the opportunity presented itself when Reds owner Sidney Weil went bankrupt during the Depression. Though Crosley enjoyed owning the team, his first love was automobiles. He built the first compact American car, calling it after himself, and there are still Crosley car collectors in the United States. (In the top photograph, he demonstrates the lightness of his car engine). He also manufactured appliances, including the famous "Shelvador" refrigerator and began radio station WLW, which for many decades had one of the most powerful signals in the country. Born in 1887, Crosley died in 1961 and is buried in Spring Grove.

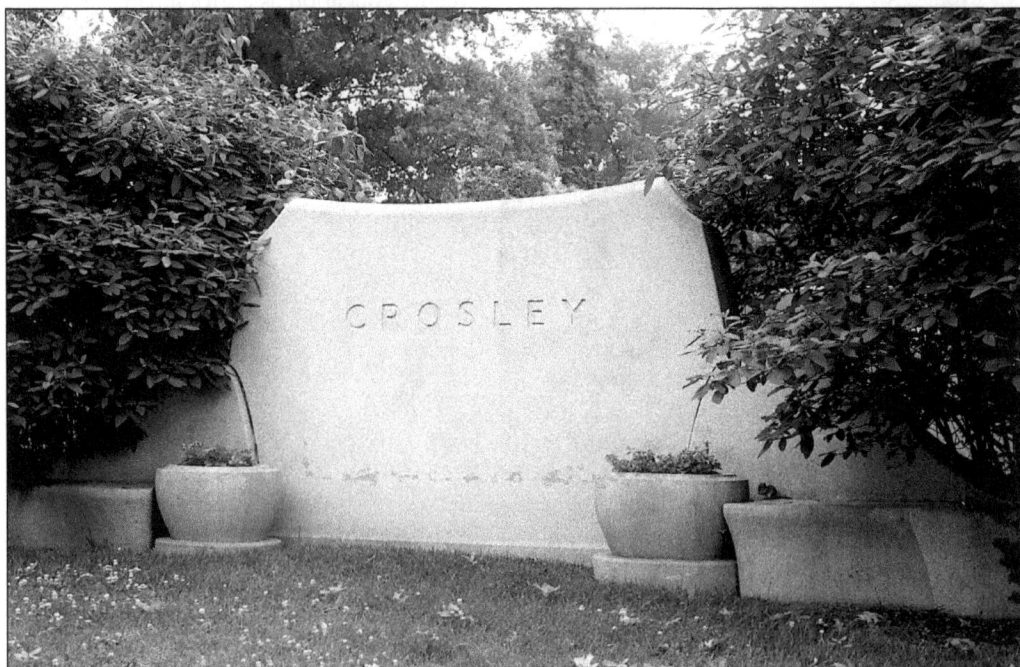

MARGARET CORNELIUS "CORA" DOW

When faced with the failure of one of the pharmacies she inherited from her father, Margaret Cornelius "Cora" Dow visualized something different for her small company. She bought and closed the equally unsuccessful pharmacy on the corner opposite her store at Sixth and Race downtown, eliminating her competition. She then installed a soda fountain and added perfume, cosmetic, and tobacco departments to her under-patronized store. This new merchandising method proved an instant success and soon competitors were copying it. Her business continued to grow, and new stores were opened in rapid succession. By 1938, there were 37 Dow Drug Company stores in greater Cincinnati, two in Springfield, Ohio, and six in Pittsburgh. Cora Dow revolutionized the corner drug store and ushered in the era of pharmacy chain stores. She died in 1915 at the age of 47 and is buried in Spring Grove.

CORA DOW

"IS DEATH THE END?
OVER THE GRAVE BENDS LOVE, SOBBING, AND BY HER SIDE STANDS HOPE AND WHISPERS: WE SHALL MEET AGAIN.
BEFORE ALL LIFE IS DEATH; AFTER ALL DEATH IS LIFE.
THE FALLING LEAF TOUCHED WITH THE HECTIC FLUSH THAT TESTIFIES OF AUTUMN'S DEATH IS, IN A SUBTLER SENSE, A PROPHECY OF SPRING."

WILLIAM HENRY ELDER

A controversial religious leader during the Civil War, William Henry Elder was the second Catholic archbishop of the Cincinnati diocese, succeeding John B. Purcell, the region's first designated archbishop and the man who founded Old St. Joseph Cemetery in 1842. Elder was born in Baltimore in 1819 and by his mid-40s was the bishop in Natchez, Mississippi. During the Civil War, he refused to allow prayers from his pulpit for either the Union or the Confederate side, believing it was not the proper role for ministers to pray for one army over another. Subsequently, he was arrested by Union troops for this refusal and jailed in Louisiana. Eventually Abraham Lincoln pardoned him. Elder was archbishop from 1883 to his death in 1904 and is buried in New St. Joseph's Cemetery.

ANDREW ERKENBRECHER

Andrew Erkenbrecher was born in Bavaria in 1821 and came to the United States with his family when he was 14. At first, the family worked on a farm in Carthage for $20 dollars a month, but as Erkenbrecher learned English, he began clerking in Cincinnati stores. Eventually he reached the point where he could buy a grain mill. The next step made his fortune: Erkenbrecher invented new methods of manufacturing cornstarch that prevented spoilage and could be used year-round. After the Civil War, he mainly used his wealth for philanthropy, and in 1875, Erkenbrecher spearheaded the creation of the Cincinnati Zoo. Ten years later, he died and is buried in Spring Grove beneath a beautiful bronze tombstone. The German inscription on the book held by the figure on his monument reads: "Death brings to an end the needs of life, but life shudders in the face of death. Life sees the dark hand, the beautiful cup that it offered."

William "Buck" Ewing was one of the best catchers of the 19th century and one of the best all-time backstops in baseball history. Born in Hoaglands, Ohio, in 1859, Buck Ewing grew up on Cincinnati's east side and first played professional baseball with Troy, New York, in 1880. Over the course of an 18-year career, he played with the New York Giants, the New York entry in the short-lived Players League, the Cleveland Spiders, and the Cincinnati Reds. He came to the Reds as a player-manager in 1895, staying with the club until the end of his career. With a lifetime batting average of .303 and a reputation of having one of the strongest throwing arms ever shown by a catcher, Ewing was elected to the National Baseball Hall of Fame in 1939. Buried in Mt. Washington Cemetery, Buck died in 1906. A reporter remarking on his life said, "He was, in his prime, in all respects, the greatest ballplayer that ever wore a spiked shoe."

Henry H. Fick

In Cincinnati's public schools, German was taught well before the Civil War, and in the decades after, German culture assumed a prominent part of the curriculum, both in language and literature and in physical education. By 1909, there were more than 180 teachers who taught German in the schools, and more than 16,000 students took instruction. Much of this activity in the early 20th century was administered by Henry H. Fick, the head of the German Department, who formed it into one of the largest in the nation. Fick's German instruction programs came to an abrupt end with the anti-German hysteria of World War I that saw German street names replaced with those of English and German-language books being taken from the shelves of the public library. His own private library became the basis of the German-Americana Collection at the University of Cincinnati. Born in 1849, Fick died in 1935 and is buried in Spring Grove. (Photograph courtesy of Don Heinrich Tolzmann.)

JULIUS FLEISCHMANN

Scion of a yeast and gin fortune, Julius Fleischmann was the Republican mayor of Cincinnati from 1900 to 1905. Although a vital part of the Cox political machine, Fleischmann was generally considered to be a reform politician, and through his social and civic connections, he was able to unify many of the factions in local politics. As a prominent distiller, Fleischmann played a leading part in the liquor interests to stave off Prohibition, but is probably best known for his ownership of the Cincinnati Reds, along with his brother Max, Garry Herrmann, and Cox. Fleischmann died in 1925 and is buried in Spring Grove in a 1913-built Doric temple mausoleum along one of the cemetery's lakes.

JOHN ISOM GAINES

Few Cincinnatians know his name today, but in the years before the Civil War, John Isom Gaines was the force behind free public education for African Americans. Born in Cincinnati in 1821, Gaines was first educated at a school run by and for former students of the Lane Theological Seminary, a hotbed for abolitionist activism. After attending the Gilmore High School, a private school for African Americans, Gaines worked as a shopkeeper and campaigned in 1849 for the Ohio state legislature to establish an African-American public school system.

For the rest of his short life, Gaines served on the Colored School Board and was its chief administrator for several years, building schools and convincing African-American families of the necessity of educating their children. He died in 1859 at the age of 38. Gaines is buried in the United African American Cemetery beneath a monument erected to him by African-American citizens in recognition for his work in promoting education and civil rights.

ALFRED T. GOSHORN

Alfred T. Goshorn was born in Cincinnati in 1833. He graduated from Marietta College and the Cincinnati Law School. Goshorn was the first president of the Cincinnati Baseball Club and was instrumental in hiring Harry and George Wright and paying the other players, making the 1869 Cincinnati Red Stockings baseball's first all-professional team. In 1870, he helped organize the city's first industrial exposition and was named president of the next three events. Due to his ability and experience, he was appointed Director-General of the United States Centennial Exposition held in Philadelphia in 1876. The exposition was judged an overwhelming success and Goshorn received medals from foreign heads of state and a knighthood from Queen Victoria in appreciation of his efforts. In 1882, he agreed to serve as the first director of the Cincinnati Art Museum, a position he held without pay until his death in 1902. He is buried in Spring Grove Cemetery.

CHARLES "CHARLIE" GOULD

Known as "Bushel Basket" for his fine bare-handed fielding at first base, Charlie Gould was the only native Cincinnati player on the fabled Red Stockings of 1869. Born in 1847, Gould played for the amateur Red Stockings in 1868 and the next year became part of the first all-professional team, a club that finished its first season with 57 wins and one tie. When the Red Stockings folded after the 1871 season, Gould played for various teams until he was named the manager of the Cincinnati Reds when the National League was founded in 1876. His first season was a disaster, the team finishing 9-56, and the next year, Gould was relieved of his duties and became a part-time player. He died in obscurity in 1917, and for decades, his grave in Spring Grove Cemetery was unmarked. In 1951, celebrating the 75th anniversary of the National League, the Reds placed a commemorative marker on Gould's grave.

HARRY HAKE SR.

A graduate of the Ohio Mechanics Institute and the Cincinnati Art Academy, Harry Hake Sr. founded one of Cincinnati's most prolific architectural firms. Born in 1871, he worked as a draftsman for several local architects before opening his practice in 1897. Hake's support of the Hamilton County Republican Party brought him many important commissions, including remodeling the County Courthouse and designing several buildings for the University of Cincinnati, and more than two dozen jobs for the city's fire and police departments. Known for his use of the neo-classical style, he designed the Western Southern Life Insurance Building (1916) and the Queen City Club (1927), both at Fourth and Broadway; the Masonic Temple and the adjoining Taft Theater (1928) on Fifth Street between Broadway and Sycamore; and the Cincinnati & Suburban Bell Telephone Company Building (1931) on the southwest corner of Seventh and Elm. Hake died September 14, 1955, and is buried in Spring Grove Cemetery.

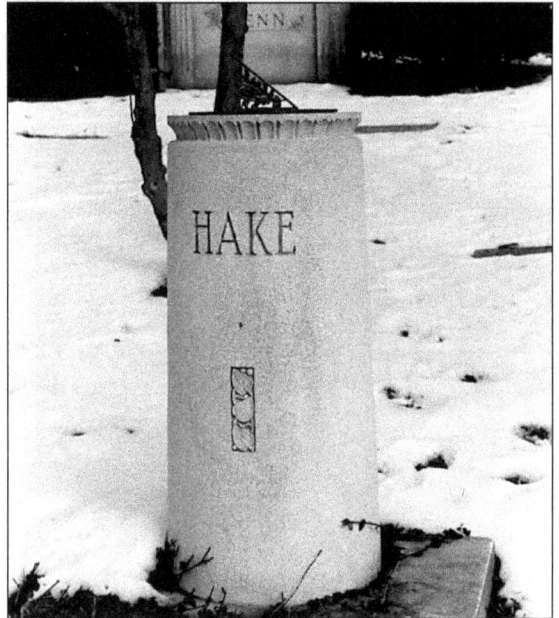

AUGUST "GARRY" HERRMANN

August "Garry" Herrmann was one of the most colorful public figures in Cincinnati history. Born to German immigrant parents in 1859, Herrmann worked as a printer's apprentice as a young man (where he acquired his nickname because he resembled the Italian patriot Guiseppe Garibaldi) and then moved up in Republican ward politics, becoming a part of Boss Cox's machine. Herrmann's jovial bon vivant lifestyle of beer, sausages, and good times and his competent genius for numbers and reports endeared him to the common man and to the reporters who covered local politics.

When he joined Cox and the Fleischmann brothers in buying the Cincinnati Reds in 1902, he became president of the club and chaired the National Commission in the Major Leagues. For two decades, he was the most powerful sportsman in the country. He is credited with being the "Father of the World Series," and he experimented with night baseball years before it became a reality. Herrmann died in 1931 and is buried in the Vine Street Hill Cemetery.

ANDREW HICKENLOOPER

Andrew Hickenlooper was born in Hudson, Ohio, in 1837. He came to Cincinnati to attend college, first at St. Xavier and then at Woodward. In August of 1861, he joined the Union Army as captain of "Hickenlooper's Cincinnati Battery." He served in dozens of battles including Shiloh, Stone Mountain, the siege of Vicksburg, and Sherman's March to the Sea. Hickenlooper reached the rank of brigadier-general before being mustered out on August 31, 1865. Returning to Cincinnati, he entered the engineering and surveying business and was appointed U.S. Marshall for the Southern District of Ohio. In 1871, he was appointed the city's civil engineer, but left that post to become vice-president of the Cincinnati Gas Light and Coke Company (now Cinergy). He later became president of the company and served in that capacity from 1877 to 1903. He also served a term as Ohio's lieutenant governor from 1879–81. Hickenlooper died May 12, 1904, and is buried in Spring Grove Cemetery.

JACOB HOFFNER

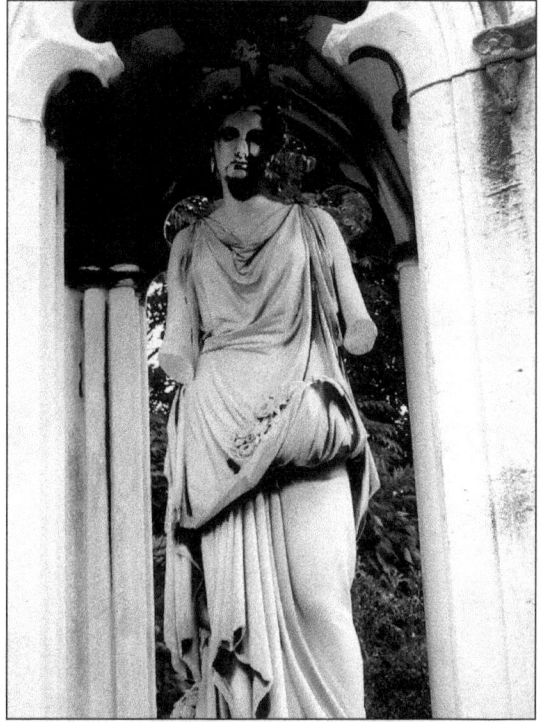

Born in 1799, Jacob Hoffner became wealthy through real estate and created fabulous gardens at his estate in the Cumminsville neighborhood. He loved to take visitors on tours of the gardens, showing them the marble lions that guarded the entrance of his property. The lions were copies of the originals that stand in the Loggia del Lanzi in Florence. When Hoffner died in 1894, he bequeathed his estate to the city of Cincinnati for a park. For 10 years, nothing was done until the University of Cincinnati board of directors was notified by the city that the lions were theirs for the taking. In 1904, the lions were placed at the entrance to McMicken Hall and have become the enduring symbols of the university. The above photograph shows the beautiful statue that graces the Hoffner family plot in Spring Grove, and the bottom photograph shows an early view of "Mick" in front of the university. "Mack" stands on the other side of the steps.

HENRY HOLTGREWE

Henry Holtgrewe was an immigrant from Hanover, Germany, who came to Cincinnati as a young man in 1885 and established himself as a saloonkeeper in the city's German neighborhoods. Known as the "Cincinnati Strongman," Holtgrewe became internationally known for his feats of strength. One time in 1904, he lifted a platform of the entire Cincinnati Reds team and their opponents, a weight of over 4000 pounds, with his back. The demonstration occurred at the Palace of the Fans ballpark. With such a man, legends and tales are bound to grow, and according to one, Holtgrewe once ripped a barbell from the concrete in front of a local theater; the owner had surreptitiously cemented it securely to the sidewalk and, offering a cash prize, defied anyone to move it. He didn't figure on the gentle giant taking him up on his offer. Most of Holtgrewe's performances were held in his saloon or in small town theaters throughout Ohio and Indiana when he toured with a vaudeville troupe, common employment for a strongman then. He died in 1917 and is buried in Old St. Joseph's Cemetery in Price Hill. (Photograph courtesy of Steven Schwartz.)

"Fighting Joe Hooker"

Known as "Fighting Joe Hooker," the Civil War general died in 1879 and is buried in Spring Grove next to his wife, Cincinnati native Olivia Augusta Groesbeck. The couple met at a ball held at the elegant Burnet House hotel when Hooker was stationed in Cincinnati. Hooker was a hero of the Mexican War, and during the Civil War, he was named commander of the Army of the Potomac. Almost 17,000 soldiers died under his command at the Battle of Chancellorsville, but the defeat did little to mitigate his military skills. Hooker, however, has come down in history for a rather dubious distinction: his allowance of women of "easy virtue" into his camps and headquarters has led such ladies of pleasure to be forever known as "hookers."

LOUIS HUDEPOHL

Louis Hudepohl was born in Cincinnati in 1842. His father ran a wholesale liquor company with George H. Kotte. Louis inherited his father's share of the business, which he and Kotte sold to buy the Buckeye Brewery in 1885. Sales increased rapidly, and 10 years later, the brewery employed 100 men and was producing 100,000 barrels of beer each year. In 1899, the company's name was changed to the Hudepohl Brewing Company. Louis loved his beer, and he also loved singing. He was a choir member at St. Paul's Church and was part of "Hudly, Midfort, and Shipley Co." (Hudepohl, Middendorf, & Schierberg), a comical singing troupe. He also served on the Board of Directors for the 1899 Golden Jubilee Saengerfest. Hudepohl died in 1902 and is buried in Old St. Joseph Cemetery. His brewery, under the capable leadership of his wife, daughter, and son-in-law, survived Prohibition and by World War II, Hudepohl was the most popular beer in Cincinnati.

MILLER HUGGINS

Called "Little Mr. Everywhere" during his playing days as a second baseman, Miller Huggins was born in Cincinnati in 1880 and educated at Walnut Hills High School and the University of Cincinnati College of Law. Huggins played for both UC and minor league teams before graduating with a law degree in 1902, and after a couple of years in the minors, played for the Reds and the St. Louis Cardinals from 1904 to 1917. It was as the manager of the mighty New York Yankees during the Roaring '20s that he made his mark, leading Babe Ruth and the Yanks to World Series championships. Now a member of the Baseball Hall of Fame, Huggins died unexpectedly in 1929 from erysipelas, a strep infection also known as St. Anthony's Fire. He was 49 years old. Huggins is buried in Spring Grove.

BARNEY KROGER

Orphaned in 1873 at the age of 13, Barney Kroger had little choice but to leave school and make his own way. After a couple of odd jobs, Kroger began selling coffee and tea door-to-door, then clerked with a tea grocer before establishing his own store in 1883 called "The Great Western Tea Company." He bought out his partner the following year, and within two years, he had a small chain of four stores. Kroger's genius was in recognizing the profits to be made by buying in bulk, advertising in newspapers, and, as he found it necessary, cutting prices to out-maneuver his competitors. He was also the first large grocer to include a bakery and a meat department in his stores. By 1893, he had 17 stores, and by 1912, Kroger had central warehouses from which he could send out his own fleet of trucks to supply his stores in small towns. Kroger died in 1938 and is buried in Spring Grove, his headstone in front of a large granite obelisk that marks the family plot.

ANNIE LAWS

Born in 1855, Annie Laws devoted her life to the cause of education, particularly as a professional opportunity for women. Laws founded the Cincinnati Kindergarten Association in 1879, an institution that eventually grew into the University of Cincinnati's College of Education in 1905. Later, it was her efforts in creating the Cincinnati Training School for Nurses that led it to becoming the university's College of Nursing and Health. Not yet finished, she also formed the School of Household Arts, which in turn became part of the College of Education with the kindergarten program.

Though a woman of remarkable achievement, she wasn't without her detractors: Annie Laws could be hard-headed and dismissive of those who disagreed with her. But her aim was to better the lives of children, and the photograph shown here of her is typical of her life. She died in 1927 and is buried in Spring Grove.

VOTE FOR

Nicholas Longworth

Republican Candidate for Re-election

=== TO ===

CONGRESS

FIRST DISTRICT OF OHIO

Deserves the vote of members of Building Associations in grateful recognition of valuable services rendered.

LONGWORTH CAMPAIGN COMMITTEE,

Fred. Otten, *President.*
Geo. W. Meier, *Treasurer.*
H. F. Cellarius, *Secretary.*

74

NICHOLAS LONGWORTH III

Born into one of Cincinnati's most prominent families, Nicholas Longworth III graduated from Harvard University in 1891 and from the Law School of Cincinnati College three years later. Election to the Cincinnati Board of Education in 1898 brought him into politics and under the watchful eye of political boss George B. Cox. Rising quickly within the ranks of the Republican Party, he was elected to Congress in 1899, where he served almost continuously until his death in 1931. During his last three terms, he was Speaker of the House. On a 1906 boat trip, he caught the eye of Alice Roosevelt, daughter of President Theodore Roosevelt. Longworth was credited with saving the life of a reporter traveling with the party who had developed a cramp while swimming and almost drowned. His bravery and good character were not lost on young Alice. They were married six months later at the White House and became the toast of Washington and Cincinnati society. Nicholas is buried in Spring Grove Cemetery.

ALEXANDER MCGUFFEY

Not as well known in the history of American education as his brother, William Holmes McGuffey, Alexander McGuffey nevertheless made significant contributions of his own. Alexander actually wrote several of the famous McGuffey Eclectic Readers, a textbook series that sold more than 125 million copies in the 19th century. Born in 1816, McGuffey graduated from Miami University when he was 16 and began teaching in Cincinnati. When William began writing the readers, his younger brother was assigned the duty of compiling the spellers, and Alexander did publish his own Eclectic Spelling Book in 1879. But for the most part, he talked little about the famous readers because he felt his contributions were little more than hired hack-work. McGuffey died in 1896 and is buried in Spring Grove.

105

JAMES W. McLAUGHLIN

James W. McLaughlin was born in Cincinnati in 1834. Wishing to pursue a career in architecture, he studied with J.K. Wilson before opening an office of his own in 1855. McLaughlin was an excellent artist and would always include human figures in his architectural renderings, giving them a unique realism and sense of scale. In 1861, he joined the Union Army and was assigned to Missouri as a bodyguard to General John C. Fremont. In 1862, McLaughlin's sketches of the war were published in *Frank Leslie's Illustrated Newspaper*. He returned to Cincinnati and to a successful career. Unfortunately, many of his buildings are no longer extant. Most are familiar with his Cincinnati Art Museum and Art Academy buildings in Eden Park, but his most architecturally important building is the former home of Shillito's (Lazarus) Department Store at Seventh and Race Streets. When designed in 1878, it was a precursor to what became known nationally as the "commercial" style. McLaughlin died in 1923 and is buried in Spring Grove Cemetery.

CHARLES McMICKEN

Nearly a century and a half after his death in 1858, Charles McMicken remains a controversial topic of discussion in the history of Cincinnati education. Born in Pennsylvania in 1782, McMicken came to Cincinnati as a young man, clerking in stores until he could establish businesses of his own. He set up as a merchant and land speculator in several states, particularly Louisiana, but acquired a reputation as "Tricky Charlie" due to his business deals. At one point in his life, he owned slaves, yet he provided land to free people of color and supported several religious denominations. The controversy surrounding him came when he died and bequeathed $1million to the city to found a university for "white boys and girls," the ultimate result of which was the establishment of the University of Cincinnati. At the city's behest, the Supreme Court overruled that clause, stating that since people of color were not specifically excluded, they were allowed to attend.

CHRISTIAN MOERLEIN

Christian Moerlein was born in Germany in 1818. Seeking opportunity, he came to this country, reaching Baltimore in 1841. He moved on to Pittsburgh and Wheeling, but since he spoke only German, he was unable to secure employment. His communication problems ceased upon arriving in Cincinnati in April 1842. He found work as a blacksmith and was soon able to open his own shop. In 1853, he relocated to Elm Street where he began a small brewery. Conrad Windisch became a partner in 1854, and the brewery prospered. Moerlein bought out Windisch in 1866. In 1870, Moerlein purchased a farm on Port Union Road in Butler County. The barley grown there, along with ice in the winter, was shipped to the brewery via the Miami & Erie Canal. By the 1890s, Moerlein was the largest brewery in Cincinnati. Its founder died in 1897 and is buried in Spring Grove. Although his company failed to survive Prohibition, the name "Christian Moerlein" lives on as a premium brew first marketed by Hudepohl in 1983.

GEORGE WARD NICHOLS

George Ward Nichols was born in Mount Desert, Maine. In 1859, he went to Paris where he studied painting under the direction of Thomas Couture. Returning to New York, he became art editor for the *Evening Post*. He entered the Union army in 1862 and was later made aide-de-camp to General William T. Sherman, accompanying him on his march to the sea. From a diary kept while in the service, he published the successful *The Story of the Great March* (1865). Nichols came to Cincinnati at the close of the war and married Maria Longworth. They envisioned a grand musical festival for Cincinnati, and in 1872, the May Festival Association was formed with Nichols at its head. The first May Festival was held in 1873 and received the acclaim of music critics from around the country. In 1879, with the financial backing of Reuben Springer, Nichols founded the College of Music. Nichols died in 1885 and is buried in Spring Grove. Much of Cincinnati's rich musical heritage can be traced to his vision and effort.

JIMMY NIPPERT

Born in 1900 to wealth and privilege as a descendant of James Gamble, the co-founder of Procter & Gamble, Jimmy Nippert was handsome, bright, and accomplished. A popular student at the University of Cincinnati, Nippert played center on the football team and was the epitome of the 1920s phrase, "Big Man on Campus." But in the traditional Thanksgiving Day game against Miami University in 1923, Jimmy Nippert was kicked in the leg. He didn't realize the seriousness of his injury at the time, so he continued to play in the game. In a freezing rain, the Bearcats beat Miami's Redskins 23-0, but shortly afterward, Nippert was admitted to the hospital. On Christmas Day, he died of blood poisoning, his last words reported to be, "five yards more to go, then drop." UC's Nippert Stadium is named in his honor.

GEORGE H. PENDLETON

George H. Pendleton is known as the "Father of the Civil Service Act." Born in Cincinnati in 1825, Pendleton was educated at the Cincinnati College under William Holmes McGuffey and astronomer/ engineer General Ormsby MacKnight Mitchel. After his schooling, Pendleton traveled widely around the world, but once back home in America, he became an attorney and then involved himself in Democratic party politics, eventually serving as a member of Congress. While involved with the Ways and Means Committee, he devised the legislation that eventually led to the Civil Service structure in the United States. He was the vice presidential candidate when George McLellan ran against Abraham Lincoln in 1864. Later a diplomat, Pendleton died in Brussels in 1899 and is buried in Spring Grove.

Elizabeth Williams Perry was born in Cincinnati in 1823. Although not herself an artist, she directed her energies to organizing women with artistic talent. From 1874 to 1877, Perry was president of the Women's Executive Centennial Committee. This energetic group decorated cups and saucers, which were sold to the highest bidders at a "Martha Washington Tea Party." The success of this event provided money to send examples of local woodcarving, china painting, and needlework to the Centennial Exposition in Philadelphia. In 1877, the committee reorganized for the purpose of establishing an art museum and art school. The Women's Art Museum Association was founded with Perry as president. WAMA sponsored art exhibits and lectures to raise awareness of the need for a museum. With the opening of the Cincinnati Art Museum in 1886, Perry ceased to be an active participant in local art circles. She died in 1914, and her cremated remains are buried in Spring Grove Cemetery.

SARAH WORTHINGTON KING PETER

Sarah Worthington King Peter was
born in Chillicothe, Ohio, in 1800. In
1816, she married Edward King of New
York, who had come to Chillicothe to
open a law practice. The Kings moved
to Cincinnati in 1831, but when her
husband died six years later, Sarah
moved to Cambridge, Massachusetts,
where her two sons were attending
Harvard College. In 1844, she married
William Peter, the British consul in Philadelphia. There she promoted cultural and educational
opportunities for women. Widowed a second time in 1853, she returned to Cincinnati where
her home at Third and Lytle Streets became a Mecca for the city's artistic and social elite.
In April 1854, she formed the Ladies' Academy of Fine Arts, which served as a springboard
for women's involvement in the arts in
Cincinnati. Sarah Peter developed an interest
in Catholicism and was received into the
church at Rome in 1855. She died in 1877
and is entombed in this beautiful mausoleum
in New St. Joseph Cemetery.

BENN PITMAN

Benn Pitman came to Cincinnati from England in 1853 to promote his brother Isaac's system of phonetic shorthand. Here he established the Phonetic Institute and published many shorthand textbooks. The Pitman method proved so useful that Benn was employed as a shorthand reporter for the judicial system. He recorded testimony at many high-profile trials, including that of the conspirators in the assassination of Lincoln. His earlier interest in art was revived by the writings of fellow Englishman and art critic John Ruskin. In 1873, he was hired to teach woodcarving at the McMicken School of Design (later the Art Academy). An exhibit of local students' work received considerable attention at the 1876 Centennial Exposition in Philadelphia. He then organized a china painting class that sparked the city's ceramics craze. Through his art and his teaching, Pitman focused national attention on Cincinnati as a major artistic center in the last quarter of the 19th century. Pitman was a founder of the Cincinnati Cremation Company, shown below.

JENNIE DAVIS PORTER

The first African-American woman to earn a Ph.D. at the University of Cincinnati, Jennie Davis Porter's 1928 dissertation was entitled "The Problem of Negro Education in Northern and Border Cities." Her writing was quite controversial, as it was viewed as an argument for segregation. A prominent educator in Cincinnati, Porter was principal of the Harriet Beecher Stowe School in the West End and advocated the idea that separate educational facilities for African American children could be culturally beneficial. She influenced generations of local African Americans with her motto, "take what you have and make what you want." Such prominent people as George Washington Carver visited her school

to observe her methods. In recent years, her dissertation has been consulted by many educators and journalists as more and more African-American academies have been created. Born in 1876, Porter died in 1936 and is buried in Union Baptist Cemetery. Her father was the first African-American undertaker in Cincinnati.

John Robinson II

Boisterous, bossy, and bedecked in loud suits, the stogie-smoking John Robinson II was the consummate circus man in the 19th century. He was born to the life. Robinson's father, the first John, ran away from his Albany, New York, home as a young man and joined a circus. It wasn't long before he had one of his own. John II was born in Alabama in 1843 when his father's circus was on tour. After service in the Civil War, he took over the circus and built it into the country's largest. The Robinson circus wintered in suburban Terrace Park, so every once in a while, a neighbor would look up and find an elephant in the yard. Before World War I, financial problems ruined the circus, and the "Governor," as he liked to be called, died in 1921. In 1874, Robinson had built a domed Moorish-Romanesque style mausoleum at Spring Grove, topped by the angel Gabriel, and there he is buried.

A.O. RUSSELL

His name may not ring a bell, but card players around the world certainly know the names of "Bike," "Bee," and "Bicycle." With partners James M. Armstrong and Robert John Morgan, A.O. Russell was the founder of what became the United States Playing Card Company, the largest and most famous manufacturer of cards in the world. "Pic" Russel was born in 1826. He met Morgan when both worked in the press room of the Cincinnati Enquirer, printing posters for the Robinson Circus, and with Robinson, the three partners formed their own printing company in 1867. By 1880, the firm was manufacturing playing cards and with other mergers, it became the United States Playing Card Company in 1894. Russell is buried in Spring Grove.

REUBEN RUNYAN SPRINGER

Son of a postmaster, Reuben Runyan Springer was born in Frankfort, Kentucky, in 1800. At an early age, he secured a job on a steamboat owned by Kilgore, Taylor, and Company, the largest wholesale grocer in Cincinnati. In January 1830, he married Jane Kilgour, daughter of the senior partner. He engaged in mercantile pursuits for the next decade and through wise investments in real estate and railroads, he amassed a sizable fortune and retired in 1840. After the 1875 May Festival, Springer proposed the construction of a new music hall to replace Saengerfest Hall and to provide a permanent home for future musical festivals and industrial expositions. To this end, he pledged $125,000 with the condition that the citizens of Cincinnati match his individual gift, which they did. He was also the primary benefactor of the College of Music, donating an estimated $200,000 toward its establishment and endowment. Springer died in 1884, but left a cultural legacy enjoyed by Cincinnatians today. He is buried in New St. Joseph Cemetery.

ADOLPH STRAUCH

Adolph Strauch was the landscape architect who created Spring Grove as a garden cemetery, following his philosophy that cemeteries must be more than acres of monuments; they must be controlled pastoral spaces of horticultural beauty as well. Strauch was born in Prussia in 1822. He was educated in botany and then became a landscape gardener in Vienna and London, eventually coming to America, and to Cincinnati in 1852. At first, he worked as a horticulturalist for local estates and through his connections with the prominent owners, was appointed in 1854 to supervise the concerted development of Spring Grove. Strauch built lakes, sculpted rolling hills, planted trees, and converted the graveyard into a remarkable garden cemetery. Strauch died in 1883 and is buried with his family on Strauch Island at Spring Grove. True to his sentiment, the plot does not include any monuments over the grave to disrupt the garden atmosphere.

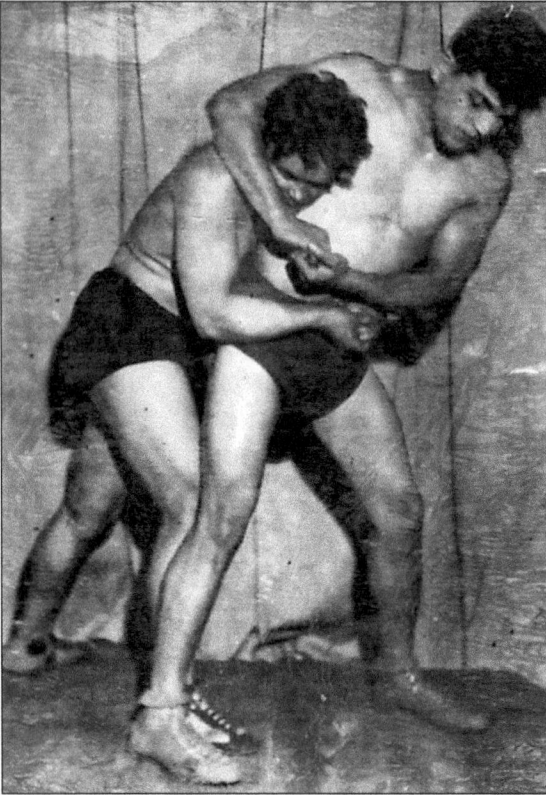

JOE WEGGESSER

At a time when the entertainment world of Cincinnati's Over-the-Rhine neighborhood included vaudeville and professional wrestling in its many theaters and arenas, Joe Weggesser, the "German Oak," was one of its stars. In Cincinnati, "Dynamite Joe" (as he was also known), would wrestle at Music Hall or Rappold's Theater. But during the Depression, he often had to travel the southern circuit, riding in a car with several other wrestlers to perform in Georgia, Alabama, and Mississippi. His most famous routine was having a group of ladies cover his thighs in lipstick kiss marks as he climbed out of the ring after a bout. After his career, Weggesser taught wrestling and refereed matches. He was born in Cincinnati in 1907 and died in 2001 at the age of 94. He is buried in Spring Grove.

MARIE "BLACKIE" WEGMAN

Marie "Blackie" Wegman was a member
of the All-American Girls Professional
Baseball League in the years following
World War II. A Price Hill native,
Wegman was a shortstop on two local
summer league teams when she signed
with the league, playing with Rockford,
Ft. Wayne, Muskegon, and Grand Rapids
in a four-year career. For the most part
playing third base, Wegman was also a
solid hitter, and one of only 550 women to have played professional ball in the league. The
circuit was started in 1943 by Chicago Cubs owner Philip Wrigley to provide some baseball
entertainment in the upper Midwest during World War II, and it lasted until 1954. Wegman
died in 2004 at the age of 78 and is buried in New St. Joseph Cemetery.

CHARLES W. WEST

Charles W. West was born in Pennsylvania in 1810. He came to Cincinnati and made his fortune in the flour industry. At the opening of the Cincinnati Industrial Exposition in September 1880, a letter from West was read in which he agreed to donate $150,000 toward the construction of an art museum, contingent upon a matching amount being raised by public subscription. Within weeks the amount had been raised. Mayor Charles Jacobs proclaimed October 9 "Museum Day," urging that it be recognized and celebrated as a public holiday. With construction money available, a site for the new museum had to be chosen. Some favored Washington Park, and others suggested Burnet Woods, but West preferred Eden Park, with its spectacular views and superior air and light. James McLaughlin was chosen to design the building, which was completed in 1886. Unfortunately, West didn't live to see the museum completed. He died in 1884 and is buried in Spring Grove under an impressive monument featuring his seated likeness on top.

HENRY WIELERT

Henry Wielert's 19th-century beer garden was a center for Over-the-Rhine German life. As the 1875 sketch (*below*) shows, it was a typical middle class hall with an orchestra and excellent food and drink. Wielert hired the Cincinnati Grand Orchestra in the 1870s to treat patrons to classical music as they enjoyed the evening. A large part of German-American culture was the hale fellow-well met atmosphere of beer halls such as his. Wielert opened his saloon on Vine Street in 1865, and it quickly became an institution. During election campaigning, Republicans found that Wielert's was the place for free beer, one of the best local brews, Hauck's, being the lager of choice. His elaborate monument in Spring Grove is topped a by a bust of the convivial saloon owner.

JOHN "SOCKO" WIETHE

John "Socko" Wiethe earned his hard-sounding nickname because of his aggression on the football field, but it later came in handy when he was just as hard-nosed in the political arena. One of the legendary athletes in Cincinnati history, Wiethe starred at Xavier University and then played for the Detroit Lions. Variously a semi-pro baseball and basketball player and a high school coach in football and hoops, Socko also worked for a time as a minor league umpire. But when Wiethe became hoops coach at the University of Cincinnati in 1946, he really made his mark. John Wiethe brought local basketball to the big time, steering his Bearcats to national exposure with a 106-47 slate from 1946 to 1952, beating some of the top teams in America. Later he became chairman of Hamilton County's Democratic Party and was a considerable force in local and state politics. Wiethe, born in 1922, died in 1999 and is buried in New St. Joseph's Cemetery.

CONRAD WINDISCH

Born in Bavaria in 1825, Conrad Windisch was a prominent brewer in the 19th century when Cincinnati boasted some of the best beer in the nation. Windisch apprenticed as a brewer under his father in his native Germany before coming to America in 1848. After working for brewers in Chicago and St. Louis, he came to Cincinnati where he finally became a brewmaster. After a brief partnership with Christian Moerlein, who would become one of the largest brewers in the country, Windisch formed a brewery in 1866 with the Muhlhauser brothers, Heinrich and Gottlieb, producing their signature Lion Lager. Windisch died on New Year's Day of 1890 and is buried in Spring Grove. Adolph Strauch, who liked the clean lines of artistic monuments, would have paled at the excess of Windisch's gravestone, a hodgepodge of funerary symbols that include Father Time, a broken oak limb, an empty hourglass, an anchor, a torch, and a harp.

GRIFFIN YEATMAN

Griffin Yeatman arrived in Cincinnati in June 1793 and built the two-story log tavern illustrated here. It stood at the northeast corner of Front and Sycamore Streets. His tavern became the center of community life in early Cincinnati. The first post office, a hospital ward, and a museum were maintained here. Yeatman's tavern also hosted many important early gatherings in its second floor meeting room. The first assembly of the territorial legislature, the first session of the Supreme Court, and in 1802, the first Cincinnati city council all met here. Yeatman died March 4, 1849, just four days short of his 79th birthday. He was buried in the Episcopal section of the Twelfth Street Burying Ground, but reinterred at Spring Grove Cemetery a year later. His son and members of the N.C. Harmony Lodge No. 2 erected the impressive Masonic column marking his grave. A horizontal brownstone slab in front of the monument covers the entrance to the Yeatman family tomb.

NOTES FOR FURTHER READING

For excellent sources on the topics of death and dying in America, see Mary Roach's *Stiff: The Curious Lives of Human Cadavers* (New York, NY, 2003), Margaret M. Coffin's *Death in Early America: The History and Folklore of Customs and Superstitions of Early Medicine, Funerals, Burials, and Mourning* (Nashville, TN, 1976), and of course the classic, *The American Way of Death* by Jessica Mitford (New York, NY, 1963). The literature on the curious history of body snatching continues to grow, and there are a number of readable and informative books. Among the best are Suzanne M. Schultz's *Body Snatching: The Robbing of Graves for the Education of Physicians in Early Nineteenth Century America* (Jefferson, NC, 1991), *Death, Dissection, and the Destitute* by Ruth Richardson (London, 1987), and James Moores Ball's *The Sack 'Em-Up Men: An Account of the Rise and Fall of the Modern Resurrectionists* (London, 1928).

For the general history of Cincinnati, two very good narratives that not only contain wonderful anecdotal accounts of local heritage, but place events and people in context are Alvin F. Harlow's *The Serene Cincinnatians* (New York, NY, 1950) and *Cincinnati Then and Now* by Iola Hessler Silberstein (Cincinnati, OH, 1982). Silberstein's work in particular, along with Zane Miller's *Boss Cox's Cincinnati: Urban Politics in the Progressive Era* (New York, NY, 1968) do an outstanding job in showing the political development of the city and the men and women who were involved in it.

Other histories worth a look because they contain profiles of prominent Cincinnatians (although they are in the manner of the late-19th-century civic "mug books") are *Cincinnati Resources* (Cincinnati, OH, 1891), George W. Englehardt's *Cincinnati: The Queen City* (Cincinnati, OH, 1901), and George Mortimer Roe's *Cincinnati: The Queen City of the West* (Cincinnati, OH, 1895). More contemporary and incisive books include a WPA guide, *They Built a City: 150 Years of Industrial Cincinnati* (Cincinnati, OH, 1938), John Clubbe's *Cincinnati Observed: Architecture and History* (Columbus, OH, 1992), *The Bicentennial Guide to Greater Cincinnati* by Geoffrey J. Giglierano and Deborah A. Overmyer (Cincinnati, OH, 1988), the reprinted *WPA Guide to Cincinnati* (Cincinnati, OH, 1987), and Daniel Hurley's exceptional *Cincinnati: The Queen City* (Cincinnati, OH, 1988).

On specific aspects of people and events mentioned in this book are Tim Holian's excellent two-volume history, *Over the Barrel: The Brewing and Beer Culture of Cincinnati* (St. Joseph, MO, 2000 and 2001), which in its discussion of brewers and brewing says so much about other facets of local heritage; Don Heinrich Tolzmann's *German Heritage Guide to the Greater Cincinnati Area* (Milford, OH, 2003), essential in outlining the contributions of German Americans to the region; and Ellis Rawnsley's *A Place Called Terrace Park* (Cincinnati, OH, 1992). Rawnsley's history of a suburban community to the east of Cincinnati gives the most concise and readable account of the John Robinson Circus.

To read about the Pearl Bryan murder case in detail, see a book written at the time, *Pearl Bryan, or: A Fatal Ending; A Complete History of the Lives and Trials of Scott Jackson and Alonzo Walling, Both Being Sentenced to Death* (Cincinnati, OH, 1896), Anthony W. Kuhnheim's *The Pearl Bryan Murder Story* (Alexandria, KY, 1996), and Anne B. Cohen's *Poor Pearl, Poor Girl! The Murdered Girl Stereotype in Ballads and Newspaper* (Austin, TX, 1973) are also helpful. Cohen's classic study traces how a local story became part of a national ballad tradition.

Otto Juettner's book *Daniel Drake and His Followers: Historical and Biographical Sketches* (Cincinnati, OH, 1909) is still the most useful reference volume for the early medical and health history of Cincinnati, almost a century after its publication. Four contemporary accounts of cholera from the 19th century are Daniel Drake's *A Practical Treatise on the History, Prevention, and Treatment of Epidemic Cholera* (Cincinnati, OH, 1832), *The Cholera in Cincinnati: Or, a Connected View of the Controversy Between the Homeopathists and the Methodist Expositor* by Samuel A. Latta (Cincinnati, OH, 1850), Orin E. Newton's book, *An Essay on Asiatic Cholera, As it Appeared in Cincinnati, O., in the Years 1849, 1850, and 1866* (Cincinnati, OH, 1867), and *Cholera in Cincinnati in 1873* by J.J. Quinn (Cincinnati, OH, 1874).

General books that are indispensable for beginning research on Cincinnati cemeteries are the 15 volumes compiled by the Hamilton County Genealogical Society, *Hamilton County, Ohio Burial Records*, edited by Mary H. Remler. Published over the years since 1984, each volume takes an individual cemetery, provides a brief history of it, and lists the burials found there. On the history of Spring Grove Cemetery, there have been many reports issued by the trustees and association over the past 150 years. One of the most useful of the early ones is *Spring Grove Cemetery: Its History and Improvements, with Observations on Ancient and Modern Places of Sepulture* (Cincinnati, OH, 1869). Don Heinrich Tolzmann has also edited a previously unpublished biography of Adolph Strauch, *Spring Grove and Its Creator: H.A. Rattermann's Biography of Adolph Strauch* (Cincinnati, OH, 1988, first written in 1905). By far, the best account of the history and design of Spring Grove is the book by Blanche M.G. Linden in 1995 as a special issue of Queen City Heritage (Volume 53, Numbers 1/2), *Spring Grove: Celebrating 150 Years*. Blanche Linden-Ward also wrote a video history of the cemetery, *Nature by Design: The Art and Landscape of Cincinnati's Spring Grove* (Cincinnati, OH, 1987). Linden-Ward is the foremost historian of garden cemeteries and her writings on Spring Grove are very well done, and outstanding sources for tracing the landscaping and design philosophies of its superintendents.

Visit us at
arcadiapublishing.com

· ·

www.ingramcontent.com/pod-product-compliance
Lightning Source LLC
Chambersburg PA
CBHW050652150426
42813CB00055B/1478